HOMELESS
IN AMERICA
HOW COULD IT HAPPEN HERE?

HOMELESS IN AMERICA

HOW COULD IT HAPPEN HERE?

Kelly Wright

INFORMATION PLUS® REFERENCE SERIES
Formerly published by Information Plus, Wylie, Texas

GALE GROUP

THOMSON LEARNING

Detroit • New York • San Diego • San Francisco
Boston • New Haven, Conn. • Waterville, Maine
London • Munich

HOMELESS IN AMERICA: HOW COULD IT HAPPEN HERE?

Kelly Wright, *Author*

The Gale Group Staff:

Editorial: Ellice Engdahl, *Series Editor*; John F. McCoy, *Series Editor*; Charles B. Montney, *Series Editor*; Andrew Claps, *Series Associate Editor*; Jason M. Everett, *Series Associate Editor*; Michael T. Reade, *Series Associate Editor*; Heather Price, *Series Assistant Editor*; Teresa Elsey, *Editorial Assistant*; Debra M. Kirby, *Managing Editor*; Rita Runchock, *Managing Editor*

Image and Multimedia Content: Barbara J. Yarrow, *Manager, Imaging and Multimedia Content*; Robyn Young, *Project Manager, Imaging and Multimedia Content*

Indexing: Susan Kelsch, *Indexing Supervisor*

Permissions: Lori Hines, *Permissions Specialist*; Maria Franklin, *Permissions Manager*

Product Design: Michelle DiMercurio, *Senior Art Director and Product Design Manager*; Michael Logusz, *Cover Art Designer*

Production: Evi Seoud, *Assistant Manager, Composition Purchasing and Electronic Prepress*; NeKita McKee, *Buyer*; Dorothy Maki, *Manufacturing Manager*

Cover photo © PhotoDisc.

ISBN 0-7876-5103-6 (set)
ISBN 0-7876-5396-9 (this volume)
ISSN 1536-5204 (this volume)
Printed in the United States of America
10 9 8 7 6 5 4 3 2 1

TABLE OF CONTENTS

Homelessness is a complex social issue. This chapter introduces the topic by outlining historical attitudes toward homelessness, explaining ways of defining homelessness and counting the homeless, and describing organizations and services devoted to homelessness.

It is difficult to count the homeless, but accurate counts are important to an understanding of the extent of the problem. This chapter relates and analyzes the results of several studies of the homeless population. Among the issues explored are the growth in the homeless population; the family structure, race/ethnicity, age, and education of the homeless; the frequency and length of periods of homelessness; and the proportion of the homeless in rural areas.

Homelessness is closely linked with poverty. This chapter defines poverty, discusses trends and forces affecting the poverty rate, and provides a statistical sketch of the poor. Employment issues, welfare reform, and the employment of the homeless are also discussed.

The primary cause of homelessness is an inability to afford adequate housing. This chapter describes the limited availability of low-income housing and the places where the homeless stay. The living situations of homeless children are also explored.

Opinions differ on the approach the government should take to alleviate the problem of homelessness. This chapter provides a timeline of government involvement, an outline of government programs aimed at relieving homelessness, and a look at federally owned and subsidized housing.

Communities often try to restrict the ways in which the homeless can use public space. Some of these restrictions may violate the rights of the homeless, who frequently lack the resources to object. This chapter outlines local regulations pertaining to homelessness, mentioning their supporters and opponents, and describes several cases in which restrictions felt to be unjust were tried in court.

Poverty and homelessness contribute to an increased risk of illness and poor health. This chapter explores the relationship between homelessness and health concerns; lists ailments common among the homeless; describes homeless populations of particular concern; and discusses the problems of providing health care to the homeless, poor, and uninsured.

PREFACE

Homeless in America: How Could it Happen Here? is one of the latest volumes in the Information Plus Reference Series. Previously published by the Information Plus company of Wylie, Texas, the Information Plus Reference Series (and its companion set, the Information Plus Compact Series) became a Gale Group product when Gale and Information Plus merged in early 2000. Those of you familiar with the series as published by Information Plus will notice a few changes from the 1999 edition. Gale has adopted a new layout and style that we hope you will find easy to use. Other improvements include greatly expanded indexes in each book, and more descriptive tables of contents.

While some changes have been made to the design, the purpose of the Information Plus Reference Series remains the same. Each volume of the series presents the latest facts on a topic of pressing concern in modern American life. These topics include today's most controversial and most studied social issues: abortion, capital punishment, care for the elderly, crime, health care, the environment, immigration, minorities, social welfare, women, youth, and many more. Although written especially for the high school and undergraduate student, this series is an excellent resource for anyone in need of factual information on current affairs.

By presenting the facts, it is Gale's intention to provide its readers with everything they need to reach an informed opinion on current issues. To that end, there is a particular emphasis in this series on the presentation of scientific studies, surveys, and statistics. These data are generally presented in the form of tables, charts, and other graphics placed within the text of each book. Every graphic is directly referred to and carefully explained in the text. The source of each graphic is presented within the graphic itself. The data used in these graphics is drawn from the most reputable and reliable sources, in particular the various branches of the U.S. government and major independent polling organizations. Every effort has been made to secure the most recent information available. The reader should bear in mind that many major studies take years to conduct, and that additional years often pass before the data from these studies is made available to the public. Therefore, in many cases the most recent information available in 2001 dated from 1998 or 1999. Older statistics are sometimes presented as well, if they are of particular interest and no more recent information exists.

Although statistics are a major focus of the Information Plus Reference Series, they are by no means its only content. Each book also presents the widely held positions and important ideas that shape how the book's subject is discussed in the United States. These positions are explained in detail and, where possible, in the words of their proponents. Some of the other material to be found in these books includes: historical background; descriptions of major events related to the subject; relevant laws and court cases; and examples of how these issues play out in American life. Some books also feature primary documents, or have pro and con debate sections giving the words and opinions of prominent Americans on both sides of a controversial topic. All material is presented in an even-handed and unbiased manner; the reader will never be encouraged to accept one view of an issue over another.

HOW TO USE THIS BOOK

It is a sad but undeniable fact that in the midst of the tremendous wealth of the United States, there are still many people who cannot afford a place to live. For some, this is a temporary condition, lasting months or years, but many who become homeless find it extremely difficult to earn enough money to afford housing again. Many organizations, both public and private, work to assist the homeless and the potentially homeless, but all studies agree that there are far more in need of help than ever receive it. This book explores these and other issues, presenting the statistics and facts that illuminate the overall state of the homeless in the United States, and the state of those programs that aid them.

Homeless in America: How Could it Happen Here? consists of seven chapters and three appendices. Each of the chapters is devoted to a particular aspect of homelessness or related issues. For a summary of the information covered in each chapter, please see the synopses provided in the Table of Contents at the front of the book. Chapters generally begin with an overview of the basic facts and background information on the chapter's topic, then proceed to examine sub-topics of particular interest. For example, Chapter 2: Demographic Characteristics of the Homeless begins by discussing the estimated number of homeless people in the United States, and the trends in the overall homeless population over time. It then moves on to a lengthy section describing characteristics of the homeless population. For instance, the level of education of homeless people, whether they are alone or part of a homeless family, and the genders, races and ethnicities of homeless people. While demonstrating that the homeless are a highly diverse population, special attention is given to segments of the overall population that are over-represented among the homeless, such as single men. The chapter then examines the typical duration of a spell of homelessness, and how likely it is that a formerly homeless person will become homeless again. The chapter concludes with a section on the rural homeless population. Readers can find their way through a chapter by looking for the section and sub-section headings, which are clearly set off from the text. Or, they can refer to the book's extensive index if they already know what they are looking for.

Statistical Information

The tables and figures featured throughout *Homeless in America: How Could it Happen Here?* will be of particular use to the reader in learning about this issue. These tables and figures represent an extensive collection of the most recent and important statistics on homelessness, housing, and related issues—for example, the percentage of the homeless who are children; how much money families of different sizes need to earn in order to stay out of poverty; the availability of low-rent housing units by region; a survey of where homeless people sleep during a typical week; and federal tax expenditures on housing, 1977–2000. Gale believes that making this information available to the reader is the most important way in which we fulfill the goal of this book: to help readers understand the issues and controversies surrounding homelessness in the United States and reach their own conclusions.

Each table or figure has a unique identifier appearing above it, for ease of identification and reference. Titles for the tables and figures explain their purpose. At the end of each table or figure, the original source of the data is provided.

In order to help readers understand these often complicated statistics, all tables and figures are explained in the text. References in the text direct the reader to the relevant statistics. Furthermore, the contents of all tables and figures are fully indexed. Please see the opening section of the index at the back of this volume for a description of how to find tables and figures within it.

In addition to the main body text and images, *Homeless in America: How Could it Happen Here?* has three appendices. The first is the Important Names and Addresses directory. Here the reader will find contact information for a number of government and private organizations that study and make public policy on homelessness. The second appendix is the Resources section, which can also assist the reader in conducting his or her own research. In this section, the author and editors of *Homeless in America: How Could it Happen Here?* describe some of the sources that were most useful during the compilation of this book. The final appendix is the index. It has been greatly expanded from previous editions, and should make it even easier to find specific topics in this book.

COMMENTS AND SUGGESTIONS

The editors of the Information Plus Reference Series welcome your feedback on *Homeless in America: How Could it Happen Here?* Please direct all correspondence to:

Editors
Information Plus Reference Series
27500 Drake Rd.
Farmington Hills, MI 48331-3535

ACKNOWLEDGEMENTS

Permission to use the following quotes, photographs, illustrations, figures, charts, and tables appearing in Information Plus Homeless in America 2001 *was received from the following sources:*

AP/Wide World Photos. Photograph of Volunteers of American serving Thanksgiving dinners. AP/Wide World Photos. Reproduced by permission.

Archive Photos, Inc./American Stock. Photograph of "Hooverville" outside a factory during the Depression. Archive Photos, Inc./American Stock. Reproduced by permission.

Association of Gospel Rescue Missions. From tables in *1999 Snap Shot Survey of the Homeless.* Association of Gospel Rescue Missions, Kansas City, MO, October 1997, and November 1999. Reproduced by permission.

Bettmann/CORBIS. Photograph of Dust Bowl, deserted farm, South Dakota. UPI/Corbis-Bettmann. Reproduced by permission.

The Brookings Institution. Haskins, Ron. "Giving is Not Enough: Work and Work Supports Are Reducing Poverty," *Brookings Review,* vol. 19, no. 3, Summer 2001. © 2001 The Brookings Institution. Reproduced by permission.

Centers for Disease Control and Prevention. From a table titled "Table 24. Tuberculosis Cases by Homeless Status: 59 Reporting Areas, 1999." Courtesy of the Centers for Disease Control and Prevention, National Center for HIV, STD, and TB Prevention, Atlanta, GA, 1999.

Cornell University Press. From tables and figures in *The State of Working America, 2000-2001.* Mishel, Lawrence, Jared Bernstein, John Schmitt, and Economic Policy Institute, November 2000. Copyright © 2001 by Cornell University. Reproduced by permission of the publisher, Cornell University Press.

Economic Policy Institute. From a figure in *Economic Snapshots.* Courtesy of Economic Policy Institute, Washington, DC, April 25, 2001.

The Gallup Organization. "What do you think is the most important problem facing this country today?" *The Gallup Poll,* Princeton, NJ, 1999. Copyright © 1999 by The Gallup Organization. Reproduced by the permission of The Gallup Organization.

National Coalition for the Homeless. From a figure in *Welfare to What? Part II.* Courtesy of the National Coalition for the Homeless, Los Angeles Coalition to End Hunger & Homelessness, on behalf of the National Welfare Monitoring and Advocacy Partnership, Washington, DC, April 19, 2001.

National Law Center on Homelessness. *Out of Sight—Out of Mind?—A report on Anti-Homeless Laws, Litigation and Alternatives in 50 United States Cities,* National Law Center on Homelessness and Poverty, Washington, DC, 1999. Reproduced by permission.

National League of Cities. From tables and figures in *State of America's Cities: The Seventeenth Annual Opinion Survey of Municipal Elected Officials.* Courtesy of the National League of Cities, Washington, DC, 2001.

National Low Income Housing Coalition. From a figure in *2000 Advocate's Guide to Housing and Community Development Policy.* Courtesy of the National Low Income Housing Coalition, Washington, DC, 2000. From a table in *Out of Reach, September 1999: The Gap Between Housing Costs and Income of Poor People in the United States.* Courtesy of the National Low Income Housing Coalition, Washington, DC, September 1999. From a table in *Out of Reach, September 2000: The Growing Gap Between Housing Costs and Income of Poor People in the United States.* Courtesy of the National Low Income Housing Coalition, Washington, DC, September 2000.

The United States Conference of Mayors. From tables in *A Status Report on Hunger and Homelessness in America's Cities, 2000: A 25-City Survey, December 2000.* Courtesy of The United States Conference of Mayors, Washington, DC.

Urban Institute. From a figure in *1999 Snapshots of America's Families II: Children's Behavior and Well-Being.* Courtesy of Urban Institute, Washington, DC, 2000. From a table in *1999 Snapshots of America's Families II: Key Findings by Race and Ethnicity.* Courtesy of Urban Institute, Washington, DC, 2000. From tables and figures in *America's Homeless II: Populations and Services: National Survey of Homeless Assistance.* Courtesy of Urban Institute, Washington, DC, February 1, 2000. From a figure in *Federal Expenditures on Children: 1960–1997.* Courtesy of Urban Institute, Washington, DC, April 2001. From tables and figures in *Homelessness: Programs and the People They Serve: Findings of the National Survey of Homeless Assistance Providers and Clients.* Courtesy of Urban Institute, Washington, DC, December 1999. From a figure in *National Survey of America's Families: 1999 Snapshots of America's Families II.* Courtesy of Urban Institute, Washington, DC, 2000. From a figure in *New Federalism: National Survey of America's Families.* Courtesy of Urban Institute, Washington, DC, April 2001. From a table in *On the Bottom Rung: A Profile of Americans in Low-Income Working Families.* Courtesy of Urban Institute, Washington, DC, October 2000.

U.S. Census Bureau. From tables and figures in *Current Population Survey.* Courtesy of the U.S. Census Bureau, Washington, DC.

From a table titled "Preliminary estimate of weighted average poverty thresholds for 2000." Courtesy of the U.S. Census Bureau, Washington, DC, January 24, 2001.

U.S. Department of Education. From tables in *Education for Homeless Children and Youth Program: Report to Congress, Fiscal Year 1997*. Courtesy of the U.S. Department of Education, Washington, DC, 1997.

U.S. Department of Housing and Urban Development. From a table in *The 1998 National Symposium on Homelessness Research*. Courtesy of the U.S. Department of Housing and Urban Development, Washington, DC. From figures in *Rental Housing Assistance—The Worsening Crisis: A Report to Congress on Worst Case Housing Needs*. Courtesy of the U.S. Department of Housing and Urban Development, Washington, DC, March 2000.

U.S. Department of Labor. From a figure in *Monthly Labor Review*. Courtesy of the U.S. Department of Labor, Bureau of Labor Statistics, April 26, 2001. From a table titled "Wage and salary workers paid hourly rates with earnings at or below the prevailing Federal minimum wage by occupation and industry." Courtesy of the U.S. Department of Labor, Bureau of Labor Statistics, Employment and Earnings, January 2001.

U.S. General Accounting Office. From a figure in *Health Insurance Characteristics and Trends in the Uninsured Population*. Courtesy of the U.S. General Accounting Office, Washington, DC, March 13, 2001. From a table in *Homelessness: Consolidating HUD's McKinney Programs*. Courtesy of the U.S. General Accounting Office, Washington, DC, May 23, 2000.

CHAPTER 1

THE NATURE OF HOMELESSNESS

From ancient Mesopotamia to 21st century Detroit, homeless people have lived among us, accepting our castoffs, sleeping on the streets. In order to understand a culture that is defined by a lack of something—in this case, a permanent place to live—one must also explore the lives of the people who have what the others lack. Social researchers—educators, sociologists, economists, political scientists—have studied homelessness in the past and present and determined that it is not so much a characteristic of certain types of people as it is an ailment belonging to certain types of societies. Social factors, especially poverty and a lack of affordable housing, are what tend to drive people into poverty, not any special traits or weaknesses of the homeless people themselves. Homelessness is in many ways just a symptom of extreme poverty.

HISTORICAL ATTITUDES TOWARD THE HOMELESS

While most experts today see homelessness as the result of how society is structured, this was not always the case. Throughout most of history, those who had homes saw most homeless people as deserving of their fate. It was assumed that the homeless were too lazy to earn a living, or that they preferred begging and not having a home to a normal life, or simply that the homeless had done something bad.

There were exceptions. The English Poor Laws of 1601 distinguished between the "worthy" and "unworthy" poor. The so-called worthy poor—widows, the elderly, the disabled, and children—were not seen as responsible for their poverty and homelessness, and might receive aid if any were available. The rest of the homeless, however, were still considered to be bad people, idlers or criminals, deserving of nothing but contempt.

When the English colonists came to North America, they brought their beliefs about poverty and homelessness with them. Some people did think that society should intervene to reduce homelessness, but they still believed that for most people homelessness was due to a weak or flawed character. So they established poorhouses, where the homeless and those who were unable to care for themselves would be sent and made to do difficult, unpleasant work. The hope was that this would reform these supposedly lazy people and convince them to get regular jobs. The people who established and ran the poorhouses did not understand that the vast majority of homeless people are homeless not out of choice, but because they couldn't find work that paid them enough to afford a house.

Poorhouses failed to reduce homelessness and had gone out of use by the early 1900s. By this time the United States was a place of increasing urbanization and industrialization. Many factory workers received little pay for their long hours, however, and housing could be hard to find in the booming cities. Homelessness became ever more common and was more and more concentrated in the cities.

It was also during the early part of the 20th century that attitudes toward the homeless began to slowly shift. Social scientists began to systematically study and interview homeless people for the first time. They discovered that, contrary to their expectations, most homeless people seemed to want to work and earn enough money to pay for housing and other things, rather than beg, steal, and do whatever else they could to survive in the streets. It was just that they couldn't find work, or the work that was available didn't pay enough for them to afford housing.

Attitudes changed even more during the Great Depression (1929–1934). After the great stock market crash of 1929, Americans faced a decade of hard times worse than anything they had known before. Millions of people lost their jobs and homes, and most of those who still had work struggled to make ends meet. A terrible drought struck the middle of the United States in the 1930s, destroying the homes and livelihoods of millions of farmers and sending them out of the so-called Dust Bowl that the Plains states

FIGURE 1.1

An abandoned farm house in South Dakota, in 1933. The great drought of this period ruined thousands of farms such as this one and added to the already enormous number of people driven into poverty and homelessness by the Great Depression. *(Source: Corbis Corporation, Bellevue.)*

had become. (See Figure 1.1.) Under these circumstances, it was easy to understand how good people, through no real fault of their own, could end up homeless. More than ever before, people felt that the government should help the homeless and poor. Many people were angry with President Hoover because he felt that the government should minimize its involvement, and he lost his 1932 reelection campaign as a result. (See Figure 1.2.)

The subsequent Franklin Roosevelt administration, as part of its New Deal program, passed many laws intended to reduce homelessness and poverty. The Social Security Act of 1935 was particularly important, as it established programs to provide government funds directly to the elderly and to children of single mothers—two groups that had always suffered greatly from poverty and homelessness. The United States Housing Act of 1937 was also of great importance. Under this law federal government programs were established to develop housing projects and to help low-income people get home loans.

The New Deal laws marked a great turning point in attitudes toward the homeless and the poor. They were

FIGURE 1.2

So many people became homeless during the Great Depression that entire towns of cheaply thrown together, unsanitary shacks sprung up, generally near factories and major cities. These shanty towns developed the nickname "Hoovervilles," as a criticism of President Hoover's unwillingness to involve the government in helping the jobless or homeless. *(Source: Archive Photos, Inc.)*

strengthened in the 1960s by further legislation, especially the formation of the Department of Housing and Urban Development in 1965. With these laws and organizations in place, American society acknowledged that people could become poor and homeless because of circumstances beyond their control, and that the government should help these people. This basic idea has continued to guide government thinking into the 21st century, although policies have changed over the years. Government concern about the plight of the poor and homeless fell, relative to other political issues, during the 1970s and early 1980s, and funding for many programs was cut or frozen. The late 1980s and early 1990s saw renewed interest in the problem, and new theories also arose about how best to help those in need. Most notably, an increasing emphasis was placed on the idea that direct government aid should be for the short term only. Steps were taken in the 1990s to try and ensure that those using various forms of welfare would seek jobs as quickly as possible.

DEFINING HOMELESSNESS

A Legislative Definition

During a period of growing concern about homelessness in the mid-1980s, the first major piece of federal legislation aimed specifically at helping the homeless was adopted: the Stewart B. McKinney Homeless Assistance Act of 1987. Part of the act laid out the official government definition of a homeless person:

An individual who lacks a fixed, regular, and adequate nighttime residence [or]

An individual who has a primary nighttime residence that is:

A. A supervised or publicly operated shelter designed for temporary living accommodations (including welfare hotels, congregate shelters, and transitional housing for the mentally ill);

B. An institution that provides a temporary residence for individuals intended to be institutionalized; or

TABLE 1.1

Common methods for collecting planning information

Method	Usual places to find people for study	Usual period of data collection and of estimate	Probable complexity of data collected
Full counts and other non-probability methods			
Analysis of agency records	Specific agency	Varies; usually not done to develop a population estimate	Whatever the agency routinely records in its case documents
Simple count, involving significant amounts of data by observation or from minimal agency records (e.g., Boston, Nashville, Minnesota quarterly shelter survey)	Shelters, streets	1 night; point-in-time estimate	Enumeration, + very simple population characteristics (gender, adult/child, race)
Simple count with brief interview (e.g., Pasadena, Colorado)	Shelters, meal programs, streets	1 night; point-in-time estimate	Enumeration + basic information as reported by respondent
Screener, counts and brief interviews for anyone screened in, plus unduplication using unique identifiers (Kentucky)	Service agencies of all types	Several weeks or months; point-in-time and period prevalence estimate	Enumeration + basic information as reported by respondent
Complete enumeration through multiple agency search and referral (Ohio, First et al.), followed by extensive interview (also unduplication)	Service agencies and key informants	Several weeks or months; point-in-time and period prevalence estimate	Usually extensive
Probability-based methods			
Block probability with substantial interview (e.g., Rossi, Vernez et al., DC*MADS)	Streets	Several weeks or months; point-in-time estimate	Usually extensive
Other probability approaches	Abandoned buildings, conventional housing in poor neighborhoods	Several days or weeks; point-in-time estimate	Enumeration + basic information as reported by respondent
Service-based random sampling (e.g., Rossi; UI 1987; DC*MADS; NSHAPC)	Usually homeless assistance programs	Several weeks, months, or years; point-in-time estimate	Usually extensive
Shelter and other service tracking systems that allow unduplication across all services in a jurisdiction over time	Service agencies	Ongoing; point-in-time or period prevalence for periods of any length	Whatever the system collects, but usually simple data for administrative purposes
Other interesting methods			
Surveys of the housed population (e.g., Link)	At home	Multi-year; produces period prevalence for periods asked about	Basic information as reported by respondent
Longitudinal studies (e.g., in Los Angeles, Oakland, Minneapolis, New York City)	Shelters, soup kitchens, streets	Multi-year; does not produce a population estimate	Extensive information, collected from the same person at several points in time

SOURCE: Martha R. Burt, "Demographics and Geography: Estimating Needs," in *The 1998 National Symposium on Homelessness Research*, U.S. Department of Housing and Urban Development and the U.S. Department of Health and Human Services, August 1999

C. A public or private place not designed for, or ordinarily used as, a regular sleeping accommodation for human beings.

A Problem Definition

There are many who disagree with the government's definition of a homeless person. Many of them feel that the definition should be broadened to include groups of people who, while they may have somewhere to live, do not really have a home in the conventional sense. Considerable debate has resulted over expanding the classification to include people in situations such as these:

- People engaging in prostitution who spend each night in a different hotel room, paid for by clients.

- Children in foster or relative care.

- A family or single person who lives with their parents, with no clear expectation of when the arrangement will end, because they cannot afford their own home.

- People living in stable but inadequate housing (having no plumbing or heating, for example).

- People doubled up in conventional dwellings for the short term.

- People in hotels paid for by vouchers to the needy.

- Elderly people living with family members because they cannot afford to live elsewhere.

The importance of defining the homeless is critical to the health of society. Because these data form the basis of the distribution of billions of dollars in federal funding for relief programs, people who are in genuine need, but excluded from the official definition, are denied help.

COUNTING THE HOMELESS

Methodology

An accurate count of the U.S. homeless population has proved to be a problem for statisticians. The most formidable obstacle is the nature of homelessness itself. Typically, researchers contact people in their homes, through in-person or telephone surveys, to obtain information regarding income, education levels, household size, ethnicity, and so forth. Since homeless people, by the very definition of their living status, are unable to be contacted in this manner, researchers have had to develop new methods for collecting data on these transient social groups. Martha Burt, Ph.D., a lead researcher with the U.S. Department of Housing and Urban Development (HUD) and the U.S. Department of Health and Human Services (DHHS) has explored this issue and published a table of the most common methods of data collection for homeless people. (See Table 1.1.) Of the methods outlined in Table 1.1, the survey methods most frequently used in homeless studies are:

- Point-in-time counts—count people who are literally homeless on a given day or week. This method provides a "snapshot" picture of the homeless.

- Full counts and nonprobability methods—count each person to be represented. The census is an example of this survey instrument, as it is designed for every single U.S. resident to respond.

- Longitudinal studies—follow specific people over a period of time to determine if they became homeless during that period of time.

- Records of local service providers, such as shelters and social service agencies.

COMPARING METHODS AND RESULTS. As Table 1.1 reveals, methods vary greatly in design and scope. This can be a problem when the results of one study contradict those of another of similar intent. Two different methodologies can show two different sets of results for the same target group. Take, for example, the statistics released by the Association of Gospel Rescue Missions as part of their *1999 Snap Shot Survey of the Homeless,* as compared with *Homeless Programs and the People They Serve: National Survey of Homeless Assistance Providers and Their Clients,* a similar study conducted by the Urban Institute in 1996.

Table 1.2 is an example of the "probability-based" method of data collection. This method attempts to count all the people receiving homeless services during one specific night and then draw conclusions about the entire homeless population from it. This is considered a "snapshot" method of evaluation—one that presents a picture of the conditions that exist at that given moment, but does not count each and every person in the larger body of the studied population. However, since current research indicates that homelessness is largely a temporary or situational condition, and since individual living circumstances are subject to fluctuation, the accuracy of this representation is frequently debated.

TABLE 1.2

1999 Snap Shot Survey of the homeless

	1999	1998
Gender		
Male	77%	78%
Female	23%	22%
Age Groups		
Under 18	11%	12%
18-25	10%	10%
26-35	21%	23%
36-45	29%	30%
46-65	24%	21%
65+	5%	5%
Race/Ethnic Groups		
Caucasian	42%	40%
Afro-American	39%	42%
Hispanic	14%	12%
Asian	1%	2%
Native American	4%	5%
Families Served		
Couples	12%	12%
Women with children	67%	66%
Men with children	5%	7%
Intact families	16%	16%
Other Information		
Veterans - Male	30%	32%
Veterans - Female	3%	4%
Served in Korea	16%	8%
Served in Vietnam	38%	42%
Served in Persian Gulf War	8%	8%
Homeless less than 1 year	69%	61%
Never before homeless	33%	N/A
Homeless once before	29%	N/A
Homeless twice before	17%	N/A
Homeless 3 or more times before	20%	N/A
More than 6 month resident of city	76%	72%
Unemployed in last 6 months	54%	52%
Lost government benefits last 12 months	17%	22%
Prefer programs with spiritual emphasis	81%	79%
In long-term rehab - Male	30%	32%
In long-term rehab - Female	19%	25%

SOURCE: *1999 Snap Shot Survey of the Homeless*, Association of Gospel Rescue Missions, Kansas City, MO, November 1999

The Urban Institute study used several different survey methods. A sample of 76 geographical areas was selected as representative of the whole of service providers in the United States. (See Table 1.3.) This is another example of the service-based random sampling as used in the Association of Gospel Rescue Missions survey. Yet the Urban Institute study also uses U.S. Census information to represent the adult population figures. Census data is gathered by directly counting everyone (or at least everyone the census takers can find). This is a full-count, nonprobability method.

Comparing the results in the "females" category of the 1999 column of Table 1.2 with the same information in the first column of Table 1.3 shows different results for what is presumably the same group, at roughly the same period of time. The Association of Gospel Rescue Missions study states that 23 percent of the homeless people in the United States are females. The Urban Institute study reports this same population subgroup is 32 percent of the total homeless population. Yet both studies have to be considered valid. Their different results reflect the

TABLE 1.3

Basic demographic characteristics, by homeless status, 1996

	Currently Homeless Clients (N = 2938)	Formerly Homeless Clients (N = 677)	Other Service Users (N = 518)	U.S. Adult Population (1996)
Sex				
Male	68(%)	54(%)	39(%)	48(%)
Female	32	46	61	52
Race/Ethnicity				
White non-Hispanic	41	46	54	76
Black non-Hispanic	40	41	32	11
Hispanic	11	9	11	9
Native American	8	2	1	1
Other	1	2	1	3
Age				
17	1	0	1	NA
18–21	6	2	4	7
22–24	5	2	5	5
25–34	25	17	12	21
35–44	38	36	18	22
45–54	17	26	16	17
55–64	6	11	16	11
65 and older	2	6	29	17
Education/Highest Level of Completed Schooling				
Less than high school	38	42	49	18
High school graduate/G.E.D.	34	34	32	34
More than high school	28	24	19	48
Marital Status				
Never married	48	45	28	23
Married	9	9	22	60
Separated	15	14	10	a
Divorced	24	25	15	10
Widowed	3	6	25	7
Living Situation				
Client ages 17 to 24				
Clients in families				
Men	*	*	*	NA
Women	3	1	4	
Single clients				
Men	5	2	2	
Women	4	1	2	
Client ages 25 and older				
Clients in families				
Men	2	3	2	
Women	9	13	14	
Single clients				
Men	62	50	34	
Women	16	30	42	
Veteran Status	**23**	**22**	**14**	**13**

Note: Numbers do not sum to 100 percent due to rounding.
*Denotes values that are less than 0.5 but greater than 0 percent.
a Included in "married."

SOURCE: "Table 3.1: Basic demographic characteristics, by homeless status" in *Homelessness: Programs and the People They Serve: Findings of the National Survey of Homeless Assistance Providers and Clients*, Urban Institute, December 1999

great difficulty of studying the homeless, not flaws in the studies themselves. The difficulty of accurately counting the homeless means that the exact size of the homeless population is very controversial.

The Official Count: the U.S. Census Survey

The official U.S. Census, which takes place every 10 years, is intended to count everyone in the United States. The results of the census are critical in determining how much federal money goes into different programs and regions of the country, as well as how many representatives each state gets in Congress. Since the U.S. Bureau of the Census takes a population census by counting people where they live, the homeless, who do not live anywhere specific, are difficult to count.

A PROBLEM OF METHODOLOGY. In 1990 census officials, on what was known as Shelter and Street Night, or S-Night, counted homeless persons in the following locations:

- Emergency shelters for the homeless.

- Preidentified street locations.

- Youth shelters.

- Shelters for abused women.

The results of this count were released the following year, categorized under the heading, "Count of Persons in Selected Locations Where Homeless Persons are Found." The methods and results received criticism from homeless advocacy groups for being inadequate and proving a low estimate of homeless people in the United States. In response, a spokesman for the Bureau of the Census, in a 1991 press release, emphasized that "S-Night was not intended to, and did not, produce a count of the 'homeless' population of the country." S-Night results were not a reflection of the prevalence of homelessness over a given year, but rather a count of homeless persons identified during a single night: namely, a point-in-time study.

CENSUS ACCUSED OF UNCONSTITUTIONALITY. The National Law Center on Homelessness and Poverty alleged that the methodology of the S-Night count was unconstitutional. In 1992 the National Law Center on Homelessness and Poverty, the U.S. Conference of Mayors, the cities of Baltimore and San Francisco, 15 local homeless organizations, and 7 homeless people (the plaintiffs) filed suit in the federal district court in Washington, D.C. They charged the Census Bureau with excluding segments of the homeless population in the 1990 population count by not counting those in hidden areas and by not allocating adequate funds for S-Night.

In its suit, the Law Center cited an internal Census Bureau memorandum that stated, in part, "We know we will miss people by counting the 'open' rather than 'concealed' (two studies showed that about two-thirds of the street population sleep concealed)." Studies funded by the Census Bureau indicated that up to 70 percent of the homeless street population in Los Angeles were missed, as were 32 percent in New Orleans, 47 percent in New York City, and 69 percent in Phoenix. Advocates were greatly concerned that this underrepresentation would negatively affect the funding of homeless initiatives.

In 1994 the district court dismissed the case, ruling that the plaintiffs' case was without merit. The court ruled that failure to count all the homeless was not a failure to perform a constitutional duty, as the Constitution does not provide individuals with a right to be counted or a right to a perfectly accurate census. The court stated that the "methods used by the bureau on S-Night were reasonably designed to count as nearly as practicable all those persons residing in the United States and, therefore, easily pass constitutional muster."

CENSUS 2000 LIMITS INFORMATION. For the year 2000 census, an operation called Service-Based Enumeration (SBE) was undertaken. From March 27th to March 29th, 2000, census workers focused solely on counting the homeless population at the locations where they were most likely to be found. For the SBE, the U.S. Census Bureau released the following schedule:

- Monday, March 27, 2000—Emergency and transitional shelters, hotels, motels, or other facilities. Enumerators will leave blank questionnaires for residents who usually stay at the shelter, but who are away at the time of the enumeration.

- Tuesday, March 28, 2000—Soup kitchens, regularly scheduled mobile food vans.

- Wednesday, March 29, 2000, from 4 A.M. to 7 A.M. only—Outdoor locations. Census workers will complete the census forms for each person at an outdoor location.

The SBE methods were considered an improvement over the methods used in the 1990 census survey. Homeless citizens and advocates alike expected to see an increase in the numbers representing the homeless, and along with those increased figures, to receive better funding. Those expectations were not fulfilled, however.

An Associated Press story dated June 27, 2001, reported that the U.S. Census Bureau would not be releasing a specific homeless count because of the liability issues raised after the 1990 census. The Bureau stated it will have only one category showing the number of persons tabulated at "emergency and transitional shelters." The people who were counted at domestic-violence shelters, family crisis centers, soup kitchens, mobile food vans, and targeted nonsheltered outdoor locations (i.e. street people, car dwellers, etc.) during the March 2000 SBE night will now be included in the category of "other non-institutional group quarters population." This is a broad category including many other people, such as students living in college dormitories.

According to Edison Gore, deputy chief of the Census Bureau's decennial management division, rather than release information on homeless people, a special report on people sleeping in shelters will come out in a year or so. Bureau officials said the homeless people they did find during the exhaustive, three-day SBE count are included in total population figures for states, counties, and municipalities. Researchers are concerned that the numbers teased from these data sets will be flawed.

People involved in the receipt or delivery of services to the homeless are worried that their programs would suffer from the lack of SBE night information. A detailed homeless count is essential for city officials and advocacy groups to plan budgets for shelters and other homeless

TABLE 1.4

City data on homelessness

City	Percent Increase in Requests for Emergency Shelter	Percent Increase in Requests by Families for Emergency Shelter	Shelter Beds	Transitional Housing Units	Family Break-up for Shelter?	Family Leave During Day	Percentage Need Unmet	Turn Away Families?	Turn Others Away?
Boston	10	18	same	same	yes	no	0	yes	no
Burlington	4	6	same	same	no	no	10	no	no
Charleston	na	12	same	increased	no	no	0	no	no
Charlotte	30	35	same	same	no	no	6	no	no
Chicago	2	3.1	increased	increased	no	no	1.9	yes	yes
Denver	na	38	increased	same	yes	yes	29.5	yes	yes
Detroit	22	15	increased	increased	no	no	23	no	no
Los Angeles	25	13	same	same	yes	no	36	yes	yes
Louisville	1	-2	same	same	yes	no	20	yes	yes
Miami	5	na	same	same	yes	yes	20	yes	yes
Minneapolis	28	15	increased	same	yes	yes	40	yes	yes
Nashville	15	11	increased	same	no	no	10	no	no
New Orleans	15	25	same	increased	yes	yes	15	yes	yes
Norfolk	6	-17	same	same	no	no	0	yes	yes
Philadelphia	4	7	same	increased	no	no	15	no	no
Phoenix	na	na	decreased	increased	yes	yes	66	yes	yes
Portland, Oregon	-13	-20	same	same	yes	yes	25	yes	yes
Providence	16	10	increased	increased	yes	yes	35	yes	yes
Salt Lake City	7	6	increased	increased	no	no	34	no	no
San Antonio	47	31	increased	increased	yes	yes	12	yes	no
San Diego	20	15	increased	same	no	no	0	yes	yes
Seattle	0	0	increased	increased	no	no	0	no	no
St. Louis	0.44	na	same	same	yes	yes	29	yes	yes
St. Paul	-9	-17	increased	same	no	yes	5	yes	no
Trenton	25	25	increased	increased	yes	yes	0	yes	na

na = not available

SOURCE: "City Data on Homelessness," in *A Status Report on Hunger and Homelessness in America's Cities, 2000: A 25-City Survey, December 2000*, The United States Conference of Mayors, Washington, DC

outreach programs. Results from the U.S. Conference of Mayors 2000 study illustrate the negative impact that inadequate funding can have on the delivery of human services. (See Table 1.4.) For example, Los Angeles city officials reported that service providers had to turn people away because of budget shortages. Homeless program funding for most cities is already strained. An average of 23 percent of the requests for emergency shelter by homeless people overall, and 27 percent of the requests by homeless families alone, were estimated to have gone unmet during the previous year. A census undercount would result in more unmet needs, which means more people will be hungry or homeless.

PUBLIC INTEREST IN HOMELESSNESS

Since the mid-1990s public interest in the homeless has died down. But in the mid- to late 1980s, the country showed great concern about homelessness. Public initiatives to draw attention to the cause were popular. For example, in 1986 the American public demonstrated concern over the plight of the homeless by initiating the Hands Across America fundraising effort. Some six million people locked hands across 4,152 miles to form a human chain across the country, bringing an outpouring

of national attention and concern to the issue. In 1986 popular comedians Robin Williams, Whoopi Goldberg, and Billy Crystal hosted the HBO comedy special *Comic Relief,* to help raise money for the homeless. The show was a hit and became an annual event. Magazines, art shows, books, and songs turned the nation's attention toward homelessness. Well-funded research studies came out by the dozens. The country was awash in statistical information regarding the homeless.

By 2001 one could only see *Comic Relief* in reruns, and old ones at that. The annual fundraiser ran out of steam in 1996, with the exception of one revival show two years later. The research studies that once inundated the public are outdated and have been replaced by a precious few, but some well-funded research centers and organizations are still studying the homeless population. While data from the large studies tend to take two years from survey to published results, the information provided is invaluable, especially when reliable information is in short supply.

The Urban Institute

The Urban Institute is a nonprofit policy research organization, located since 1968 in Washington, D.C. The

FIGURE 1.3

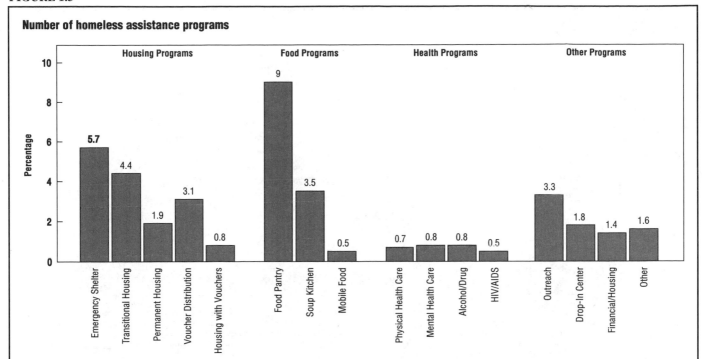

Number of homeless assistance programs

Note: Financial (usually welfare) and housing assistance services were mentioned often enough under "Other" to warrant a category of their own, and migrant housing was combined with "Other" because there were so few programs.

SOURCE: "Figure 4.1: Number of Homeless Assistance Programs in the United States," in *Homelessness: Programs and the People They Serve: Findings of the National Survey of Homeless Assistance Providers and Clients,* Urban Institute, Washington, DC, December 1999

Institute conducts research projects, publishes newsletters and books regarding social issues, and evaluates government programs. The Institute is dedicated to examining society's problems and developing methods to solve them. The Institute's work is designed to help improve government decisions and increase citizens' awareness about important social issues. The Institute's funding comes from a variety of government, corporate, and private organizations and people.

The Urban Institute study "Homelessness: Programs and the People They Serve," published in December 1999, is hailed as landmark in homelessness research. The program was designed specifically to update a 1987 Institute study. The survey is based on a statistical sample of 76 metropolitan and nonmetropolitan areas, including small cities and rural areas. It provides relevant information about homeless service providers and examines the characteristics of those who use those services. The analysis presents information about homelessness in national, urban, suburban, and rural areas. It is one of the most comprehensive research studies available today.

The United States Conference of Mayors

The United States Conference of Mayors is the official organization of the leaders of cities with populations of 30,000 or more. Over one thousand cities send their chief elected official, the mayor, to the annual conference.

Since 1982 the U.S. Conference of Mayors has conducted and published an annual survey to bring attention to the shortage of emergency services—food, shelter, medical care, income assistance—in the nation's largest cities. The survey tracks the increases or reductions in the demand for emergency services from year to year, including services for the homeless. This study has become one of the leading sources of homelessness research today.

The National Coalition for the Homeless

The National Coalition for the Homeless (NCH) is a socially and politically active group, consisting of homeless persons, activists, service providers, and people who are dedicated to ending homelessness. NCH serves as a national clearinghouse for information and works as a referral resource to enhance the public's understanding of homelessness. NCH believes that homelessness can be eliminated through public education, legislative advocacy, and grassroots movements. The group is dedicated to meeting that goal.

Other Organizations

Homes for the Homeless (HFH) is a New York City-based program designed to find long-term solutions for homeless people in New York. HFH designed an innovative and successful program, the American Family Inn, which is used as a model for permanent solutions to home-

FIGURE 1.4

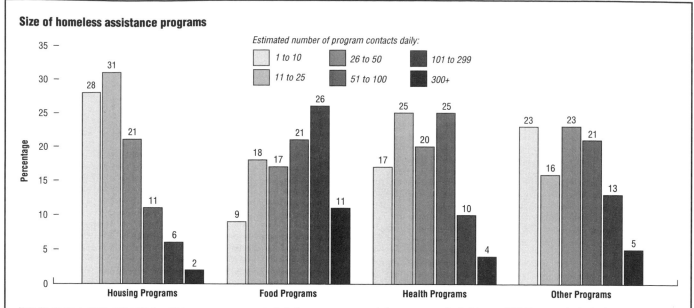

Size of homeless assistance programs

Estimated number of program contacts daily:
- 1 to 10
- 11 to 25
- 26 to 50
- 51 to 100
- 101 to 299
- 300+

Note: These are program staff estimates of how many program contacts their own program expected on an average day in February 1996. They contain duplication and cannot be added together to get the total number of people served on an average day. Housing programs include emergency, transitional, permanent housing, and voucher programs; food programs include pantries, soup kitchens, and mobile food programs; health programs include general health, mental health, alcohol/drug, and HIV/AIDS programs; other programs include outreach, drop-in centers, financial/housing assistance, and other.

SOURCE: "Figure 4.3: Size of Homeless Assistance Program," in *Homelessness: Programs and the People They Serve: Findings of the National Survey of Homeless Assistance Providers and Clients*, Urban Institute, Washington, DC, December 1999

lessness. HFH is affiliated with the Institute for Children and Poverty, and together they conduct research studies to uncover strategies for fighting poverty and homelessness.

The National Alliance to End Homelessness (NAEH) is a nationwide federation of public, private, and nonprofit organizations, operating along the assumption that homelessness can be ended. Alliance members work together, advancing the implementation of practical, community-based solutions to homelessness.

The National Law Center on Homelessness and Poverty states that their mission is "to alleviate, ameliorate and end homelessness by serving as the legal arm of the nationwide movement to end homelessness." The Law Center works to advocate effectively to protect the rights of homeless people and to end homelessness in America. The Center uses three main strategies to achieve this goal: impact litigation, policy advocacy, and public education. The Law Center conducts research studies and distributes the results by publishing fact sheets and a monthly newsletter.

HOMELESS SERVICES

A number of different organizations across the country provide services that help the homeless. Some of these programs are aimed directly at homeless people, such as shelters. Others are programs open to a wider group of needy people that includes most or all of the homeless—for example, a free clinic for the poor. Both types of programs are considered homeless services.

FIGURE 1.5

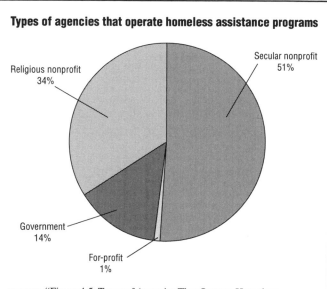

Types of agencies that operate homeless assistance programs

Religious nonprofit 34%
Secular nonprofit 51%
Government 14%
For-profit 1%

SOURCE: "Figure 4.5: Types of Agencies That Operate Homeless Assistance Programs," in *Homelessness: Programs and the People They Serve: Findings of the National Survey of Homeless Assistance Providers and Clients*, Urban Institute, Washington, DC, December 1999

Homeless assistance programs serve a great many needs, delivering services in four broad categories: housing, food, health, and outreach or walk-in services. The Urban Institute studied service providers on a nationwide level and found 16 different types of programs in these four different categories, for a total of over 39,000 home-

FIGURE 1.6

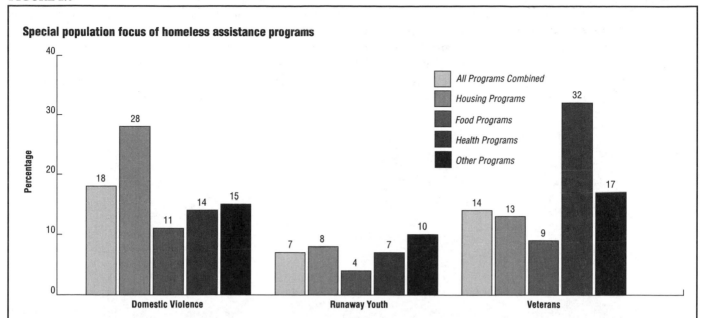

Special population focus of homeless assistance programs

Note: Housing programs include emergency, transitional, permanent housing, and voucher programs; food programs include pantries, soup kitchens, and mobile food programs; health programs include general health, mental health, alcohol/drug, and HIV/AIDS programs; other programs include outreach, drop-in centers, financial/housing assistance, and other.

SOURCE: "Figure 4.9: Special Population Focus of Homeless Assistance Programs," in *Homelessness: Programs and the People They Serve: Findings of the National Survey of Homeless Assistance Providers and Clients,* Urban Institute, Washington, DC, December 1999

less service programs in the United States. Figure 1.3 shows that food pantries were the most common service, with 9,000 in the United States. The next largest group of programs for the homeless was emergency shelters, with 5,700 available nationwide. However, the combined total of all national housing and shelter programs, 15,900, exceeded the total of 13,000 food programs.

The Urban Institute also studied how heavily used different types of homeless services were. Figure 1.4 illustrates the scope of food programs, with 26 percent of the surveyed providers expecting between 101 and 299 requests daily, and 11 percent expecting more than 300 contacts a day. Walk-in services (labeled "other" on the graph) and health programs expected roughly the same volume of clients. For example, 5 percent of walk-in programs expected over 300 people a day, as did 4 percent of health programs. Housing programs served the lowest number of people per day: on average, only 2 percent of the programs expected 300 contacts a day. This is largely due to the fact that food, health, and walk-in services (such as job counseling) are, by nature, geared toward multiple returns, whereas housing programs provide single-client service delivery over a longer period of time. Furthermore, many housing programs are geared specifically toward helping only homeless people, while many food, health, and walk-in programs are open to a wider group of people.

Most services to the homeless are a blend of federal, state, public, and private funding sources and administra-tion. Nonprofit agencies handled the vast majority (85 percent) of homeless assistance programs. (See Figure 1.5.) These programs consist of the secular, or nonreligious, nonprofits (51 percent) and religious nonprofits (34 percent). Government agencies operated 14 percent of all programs, while for-profit agencies operated only 1 percent.

Different types of agencies often specialize in particular types of service. Secular nonprofits provided much of the services aimed specifically at the homeless. They operated 60 percent of the housing programs in the United States and 43 percent of the homeless health programs. Secular nonprofits are also the most prominent type of agency among "other" homeless assistance programs, such as outreach programs, drop-in centers, and financial assistance programs. Religious nonprofits provided 55 percent of the general food programs. State and federal governments operated 51 percent of general health programs that were used by large enough numbers of homeless people to be considered homeless services. For-profit organizations play almost no role in operating homeless assistance programs (1 percent in housing, health, and other programs, and 0 percent in food programs).

Special Population Services

Many homeless assistance programs are open to anyone who wants to use them, but other programs are designed to serve only specific groups of people. The population served may be defined in several different ways: men by themselves, women by themselves, households with children, youth by themselves, battered women, or veterans, for example. The Urban Institute study revealed that less than one-third of all homeless service programs named a specific population group as a focus. Of the groups that did focus their attention on a particular part of the homeless population, programs for domestic-violence victims (18 percent of all special group programs) and veterans (14 percent) were the most common. (See Figure 1.6.) Housing programs were the most likely to name victims of domestic violence as their target group (28 percent of special programs do so). Health programs were most likely to name veterans as their focus (32 percent of all the special group programs). Only 10 percent of specially targeted programs were for youths.

CHAPTER 2
DEMOGRAPHIC CHARACTERISTICS OF THE HOMELESS

In February of 2000 Urban Institute researchers Martha Burt and Lauden Aron released a report on the state of America's homeless entitled *America's Homeless II: Populations and Services* (Urban Institute, 2000). The report, which was based on the Urban Institute's 1996 survey of the homeless population, *Homelessness: Programs and the People They Serve—Findings of the National Survey of Homeless Assistance Providers and Clients* (Urban Institute, December 1999), estimated the number of homeless people nationwide. Since the U.S. Census Bureau chose not to release a total count of homeless people in the country as of 2000, the Burt and Aron report serves an important purpose in terms of understanding the scope of present-day homelessness.

Table 2.1 indicates that the number of people who were homeless for part of 1996 was between 2.3 and 3.5 million. The table also shows that in October of 1996 the average weekly estimate of homeless people in the United States was 444,000, down from 842,000 in February of the same year. The numbers of homeless "spells" begun in a week showed a similar trend: from 52,000 people in February to 36,900 in October. The differences between February and October reflect the fact that it is easier to find and count homeless people in the winter, as they are more likely to seek help during the coldest part of the year.

AN INCREASING POPULATION

Research indicates that homelessness is growing. In 1989 the Urban Institute published a report from a national study conducted by Martha Burt and Barbara Cohen that showed the yearly national level of homelessness to be one million people (*America's Homeless: Numbers, Characteristics, and Programs That Serve Them*, Urban Institute, 1989). Compared with the figures in Table 2.1, even using the lowest projections of 2.3 million, the number of people who were homeless in the United States in a year more than doubled in less than a decade.

TABLE 2.1

Number likely to be homeless at least once in a given year

	Average week estimate	New homeless spells begun in last week	Annual projection
October 1996	444,000	36,900	2.3 million people
February 1996	842,000	52,000	3.5 million people

SOURCE: "Number Likely to Be Homeless at Least Once in a Given Year," in *America's Homeless II: Populations and Services: National Survey of Homeless Assistance*, Urban Institute, Washington, DC, February 1, 2000

Unmet Needs

A national advocacy group, The National Coalition for the Homeless, researched the increases reported in various studies from 1983 to 1996 (*Homelessness in America: Unabated and Increasing—A Ten-Year Perspective*, 1997). Most of the communities studied had doubled or tripled their shelter capacity in order to accommodate increasing numbers of homeless, but the demand for shelter space far exceeded supply.

The United States Conference of Mayors, in its 2000 survey (*A Status Report on Hunger and Homelessness in America's Cities: 2000*, Washington, D.C., 2000), did not estimate the total numbers of homeless, but it did report on the requests for emergency shelter in 25 major cities. Table 2.2 shows the results.

In 2000 requests for emergency shelter increased in the survey cities by an average of 15 percent, with 76 percent of the cities reporting an increase. The demand for shelter for entire families of homeless people was even higher, increasing by an average of 17 percent, with 72 percent of the cities reporting an increase. An average of 23 percent of the requests for emergency shelter by all homeless people went unmet. Once again, homeless

TABLE 2.2

Hunger and homelessness, 1985–2000

Indicator	1985	1986	1987	1988	1989	1990	1991	1992	1993	1994	1995	1996	1997	1998	1999	2000
Hunger																
Increase in demand for emergency food	28%	25%	18%	19%	19%	22%	26%	18%	13%	12%	9%	11%	16%	14%	18%	17%
Cities in which demand for food increased	96%	88%	92%	88%	96%	90%	93%	96%	83%	83%	72%	83%	86%	78%	85%	83%
Increase in demand by families for food assistance	30%	24%	18%	17%	14%	20%	26%	14%	13%	14%	10%	10%	13%	14%	15%	16%
Portion of those requesting food assistance who are families with children	NA	NA	67%	62%	61%	75%	68%	68%	67%	64%	63%	62%	58%	61%	58%	62%
Demand for emergency food unmet	17%	23%	18%	15%	17%	14%	17%	21%	16%	15%	18%	18%	19%	21%	21%	13%
Cities in which food assistance facilities must turn people away	67%	55%	67%	62%	73%	86%	79%	68%	68%	73%	59%	50%	71%	47%	54%	46%
Cities which expect demand for emergency food to increase next year	88%	84%	84%	85%	89%	100%	100%	89%	100%	81%	96%	96%	92%	96%	84%	71%
Homelessness																
Increase in demand for emergency shelter	25%	20%	21%	13%	25%	24%	13%	14%	10%	13%	11%	5%	3%	11%	12%	15%
Cities in which demand increased	88%	96%	96%	93%	89%	80%	89%	88%	81%	80%	63%	71%	59%	72%	69%	76%
Demand for emergency shelter unmet	NA	24%	23%	19%	22%	19%	15%	23%	25%	21%	19%	20%	27%	26%	25%	23%
Cities in which shelters must turn people away	60%	72%	65%	67%	59%	70%	74%	75%	77%	72%	82%	81%	88%	67%	73%	56%
Cities which expect demand for shelter to increase next year	88%	84%	92%	89%	93%	97%	100%	93%	88%	71%	100%	100%	100%	93%	92%	72%
Composition of homeless population																
Single men	60%	56%	49%	49%	46%	51%	50%	55%	43%	48%	46%	45%	47%	45%	43%	44%
Families with children	27%	28%	33%	34%	36%	34%	35%	32%	34%	39%	36%	38%	36%	38%	36%	36%
Single women	12%	15%	14%	13%	14%	12%	12%	11%	11%	11%	14%	14%	14%	14%	13%	13%
Unaccompanied youth	NA	NA	4%	5%	4%	3%	3%	2%	4%	3%	4%	3%	4%	3%	NA	7%
Children	NA	NA	NA	25%	25%	23%	24%	22%	30%	26%	25%	27%	25%	25%	NA	NA
Severely mentally ill	33%	29%	23%	25%	25%	28%	29%	28%	27%	26%	23%	24%	27%	24%	19%	22%
Substance abusers	37%	29%	35%	34%	44%	38%	40%	41%	48%	43%	46%	43%	43%	38%	31%	37%
Employed	NA	19%	22%	23%	24%	24%	18%	17%	18%	19%	20%	18%	17%	22%	21%	26%
Veterans	NA	NA	NA	26%	26%	26%	23%	18%	21%	23%	23%	19%	22%	15%	14%	15%

SOURCE: "Hunger and Homelessness in America's Cities: A Sixteen-Year Comparison of Data," in *A Status Report on Hunger and Homelessness in America's Cities, 2000: A 25-City Survey,* The United States Conference of Mayors, Washington, DC, December 2000 families were worse off than single homeless people, with an estimated 27 percent of their requests going unmet in 2000. Families require larger spaces and more beds in order to remain together, and many times the shelters are too full to be able to accommodate families without splitting them up. In 68 percent of the cities, emergency shelters reported that it was possible they would have to turn away homeless families because of lack of resources; 56 percent reported the possibility of having to turn away single homeless people.

Officials in 72 percent of the cities expect that requests for emergency shelter will increase in 2001. Seventy-nine percent expect that requests by homeless families will increase. People remain homeless an average of five months in the survey cities. Fifty percent of the cities said that the length of time people stay homeless increased during 2000. Officials in the survey cities report that the increase in the Department of Housing and Urban Development's (HUD) funding to address homelessness has been successful in helping homeless families and individuals into transitional and permanent housing. These officials have mixed views regarding the effect that the 2001 economy is having on the problem of homelessness.

In 2000 the National League of Cities surveyed a random sample of the nation's municipal elected officials regarding issues and problems they face in governing American cities (*The State of America's Cities: Seventeenth Annual Opinion Survey of Municipal Elected Officials,* National League of Cities, 2001). When asked to indicate whether various conditions had improved or worsened in their cities in the previous year, 10 percent of the officials reported that homelessness had worsened in their cities, while 8 percent said homelessness had improved. (See Figure 2.1.) When city officials were asked to list the top three "most deteriorated" conditions in their cities, homelessness was not even in the top ten, as it had been in previous years, but "housing" ranked second at 19 percent. (See Table 2.3.) The 2000 *State of America's Cities* survey asked respondents to characterize the situation in their cities with respect to housing affordability for low- and moderate-income households. The response: nearly three-quarters (74 percent) said there is either a "somewhat limited supply" (44.6 percent) or a "serious shortage" (29.5 percent) of affordable housing. (See Figure 2.2.) Only one in four (26 percent) responded that affordable housing was in "ample supply."

In the Conference of Mayors' survey, lack of affordable housing was identified as the major cause of homelessness in 24 out of 25 cities. Requests for rental assistance and other forms of assisted housing by low-income families and individuals increased in 68 percent of the cities during 2000. This lack of housing is of key importance in the study of homelessness. Insufficient housing options for low-income people often result in

TABLE 2.3

Most deteriorated city conditions*

Traffic congestion	49%
Availability of housing	19%
Infrastructure	16%
Cost and availability of health services	15%
Impacts of unfunded mandates	14%
Development patterns in the region	12%
Quality of education	11%
Unemployment	10%
City fiscal conditions	10%
Cable TV rates	9%
Drug/alcohol abuse	7%

*Percent of city officials listing item as one of the three most deteriorated city conditions during the past five years.

SOURCE: "Table 3. Most Deteriorated City Conditions," in *State of America's Cities: The Seventeenth Annual Opinion Survey of Municipal Elected Officials*, National League of Cities, Washington, DC, January 2001

homelessness. The city officials also estimate that low-income households spend an average of 51 percent of their income on housing. Disproportionate housing costs are another precipitating factor that bears scrutiny.

THE MANY FACES OF THE HOMELESS

Since it is effectively impossible to get a completely accurate picture of the homeless population, when discussing its characteristics it is best to look at many different studies and compare their results. Every study conducted in the 1990s and in 2000 showed that single, unattached adults comprise the largest segment of the homeless population. The 2000 study by the U.S. Conference of Mayors found this group to make up 57 percent of the total homeless population. Unattached men outnumbered unattached women by about three to one. Homeless families made up slightly more than a third of the population, at 36 percent. Most homeless families, 63 percent, were headed by only a single parent. The remaining 7 percent of the homeless population were children without any adult relatives—known as "unaccompanied youth." See Table 2.4 for a city-by-city breakdown of the homeless population.

The U.S. Conference of Mayors' study found that African Americans made up 50 percent of the homeless population, far out of proportion with their percentage of the overall U.S. population. Whites were 35 percent of the homeless population; Hispanics, 12 percent; Native Americans, 2 percent; and Asian Americans, 1 percent. Also of note in the study was that 22 percent of the homeless people surveyed suffered from a mental illness; 37 percent were substance abusers; and 15 percent were veterans. Only 26 percent had regular work at a full- or part-time job. (See Table 2.4.)

The Urban Institute's 1996 study of homelessness yielded somewhat different results than the U.S. Conference of Mayors' 2000 study, due partly to the fact that it

FIGURE 2.1

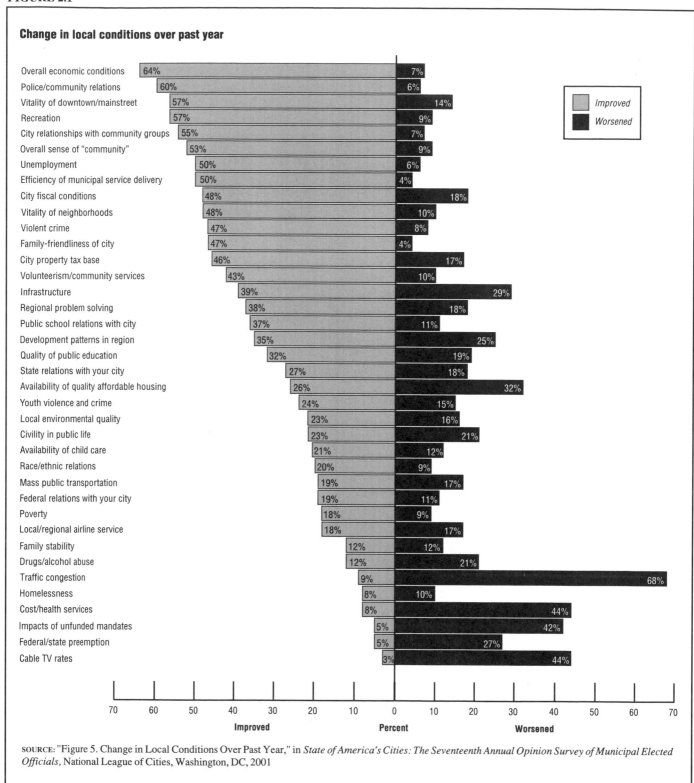

Change in local conditions over past year

	Improved	Worsened
Overall economic conditions	64%	7%
Police/community relations	60%	6%
Vitality of downtown/mainstreet	57%	14%
Recreation	57%	9%
City relationships with community groups	55%	7%
Overall sense of "community"	53%	9%
Unemployment	50%	6%
Efficiency of municipal service delivery	50%	4%
City fiscal conditions	48%	18%
Vitality of neighborhoods	48%	10%
Violent crime	47%	8%
Family-friendliness of city	47%	4%
City property tax base	46%	17%
Volunteerism/community services	43%	10%
Infrastructure	39%	29%
Regional problem solving	38%	18%
Public school relations with city	37%	11%
Development patterns in region	35%	25%
Quality of public education	32%	19%
State relations with your city	27%	18%
Availability of quality affordable housing	26%	32%
Youth violence and crime	24%	15%
Local environmental quality	23%	16%
Civility in public life	23%	21%
Availability of child care	21%	12%
Race/ethnic relations	20%	9%
Mass public transportation	19%	17%
Federal relations with your city	19%	11%
Poverty	18%	9%
Local/regional airline service	18%	17%
Family stability	12%	12%
Drugs/alcohol abuse	12%	21%
Traffic congestion	9%	68%
Homelessness	8%	10%
Cost/health services	8%	44%
Impacts of unfunded mandates	5%	42%
Federal/state preemption	5%	27%
Cable TV rates	3%	44%

Improved — Percent — Worsened

SOURCE: "Figure 5. Change in Local Conditions Over Past Year," in *State of America's Cities: The Seventeenth Annual Opinion Survey of Municipal Elected Officials,* National League of Cities, Washington, DC, 2001

was conducted a few years earlier and partly to the difficulties of studying the homeless. It found that 68 percent of homeless adults were males, down from 81 percent in a similar Urban Institute study from 1992. (See Table 1.3 in Chapter 1.) Women accounted for 32 percent of homeless adults. Families accounted for 15 percent of all the homeless people in the study.

The Urban Institute study agreed with that of the Conference of Mayors in finding that men were much more likely to be homeless and by themselves than women. The Urban Institute's study found that 77 percent of single homeless people were male, and 23 percent female—a somewhat higher proportion of men to women than the Conference of Mayors found.

When the Urban Institute investigated the education of homeless people, they found that 38 percent had less than a high school education; 34 percent had completed high school; and 28 percent had some education beyond high school. African Americans comprised 40 percent of the homeless population, once again a higher percentage than their share of the non-homeless population. Whites made up 41 percent of the homeless population, while Hispanics comprised 11 percent. Native Americans made up 8 percent of single homeless people in this study, much higher than the percentage of the total homeless population they accounted for in the Conference of Mayors' study, and much higher than their percentage of the total U.S. population. The remaining 1 percent of the single homeless population consisted of other races. (See Table 1.3 in Chapter 1.)

The Urban Institute's 1996 study also investigated the characteristics of homeless families. It found that 84 percent of the surveyed homeless families were headed by women, while only 16 percent were headed by men. The heads of most homeless families had either never married (41 percent) or were divorced or separated from their spouse (36 percent). Only 23 percent were married. African Americans also made up a higher percentage of homeless heads of families than they did of single homeless people (43 percent). Whites made up 38 percent of homeless heads of families; Hispanics, 15 percent; Native Americans, 3 percent; and other races, 1 percent.

Since 1989 the Association of Gospel Rescue Missions (AGRM) has annually surveyed over one hundred rescue missions. Its 1999 *Snap Shot Survey of the Homeless Association of Gospel Rescue Missions* (November 1999) is similar in its methodology to the 1996 Urban Institute study. It found that 77 percent of all homeless people were men, and 23 percent were women. Children made up 11 percent of the population surveyed. (See Table 1.2 in Chapter 1.)

When the AGRM looked at homeless families, it found that 67 percent consisted of single women with children, while only 5 percent consisted of single men with children. Another 16 percent were completely intact families with children, while 12 percent were couples with no children. (See Table 1.2 in Chapter 1.)

AGRM also reported that African Americans made up 39 percent of shelter clients in 1999 (down 3 percent from the previous year); whites, 42 percent (up 2 percent from the previous year); Hispanics, 14 percent (up 2 percent from the previous year); Native Americans, 4 percent (down 1 percent from the previous year); and Asians, 1 percent (down 1 percent from the previous year). (See Table 1.2 in Chapter 1.)

Family Structure

The three major studies of the homeless discussed above have their differences, but they also agree on many

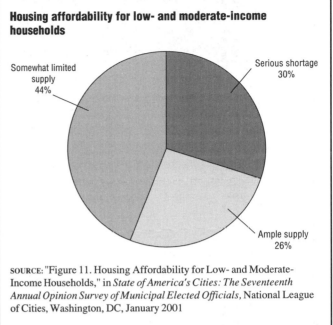

FIGURE 2.2

Housing affordability for low- and moderate-income households

Somewhat limited supply 44%

Serious shortage 30%

Ample supply 26%

SOURCE: "Figure 11. Housing Affordability for Low- and Moderate-Income Households," in *State of America's Cities: The Seventeenth Annual Opinion Survey of Municipal Elected Officials,* National League of Cities, Washington, DC, January 2001

points. One is that most homeless people are by themselves. This is especially true of men, who make up the largest part of the homeless population.

In 2000 the U.S. Conference of Mayors reported that homeless families with children comprised 36 percent of the homeless population across the surveyed cities. (See Table 2.2.) This shows a 2 percent drop from the 1998 study, but a 9 percent increase from 1985. The AGRM study and the Urban Institute study both found that single women are the heads of the vast majority of homeless families with children. The fact that men make up a larger overall percentage of the homeless population than women demonstrates just how strong this concentration is, and makes clear that a large percentage of all the women who are homeless have children with them. There are many trends that contribute to these statistics, including the fact that women tend to take care of children in the United States, yet they also tend to earn less money than men. Thus, single women with children are particularly vulnerable to poverty and homelessness.

HOMELESS CHILDREN. In the 1996 Urban Institute study, it was estimated that roughly 38 percent of all the people who were homeless that year were children. (See Figure 2.3.) This includes both children in families and children who were homeless and alone ("unaccompanied youth"). The Department of Education conducted a state-by-state count of homeless children in school in 1997. The results showed a total of 625,330 homeless children for the reporting states. (All but four states reported.) These figures do not account for homeless children younger than school age or those not enrolled because of

TABLE 2.4

Composition of the homeless population

City	Families	Men	Women	Youth	African-American	White	Hispanic	Asian	Native American	Mentally Ill	Substance Abusers	Employed	Veterans	Single Parent Families	Family Members who are Children
Boston	0	0	0	0	38	43	17	1	1	23	35	13	17	94	62
Burlington	37	35	9	19	9	85	3	1	2	40	28	17	15	50	67
Charleston	28	58	14	0	69	26	5	0	0	41	79	67	31	82	33
Charlotte	34	34	26	6	72	23	3	1	1	0	0	8.3	0.8	36	39
Chicago	45	33	15	0	79	11	9	0.4	0.3	8.4	38	23	14	96	68
Denver	49	63	15	3	20	52	20	1	7	24	29	0	27	82	62
Detroit	26	52	7	4	89	7	3	1	0	25	52	10	33	18	80
Los Angeles	16	60	22	10	58	14	23	3	2	20	40	21	23	49	34
Louisville	18	64	16	6	49	47	3	1	1	23	32	8	16	0	11
Miami	23	32	13	0	61	41	23	0.01	0.01	45	69	35	13	77	66
Minneapolis	25	71	17	26	42	30	13	3	12	32	74	50	22	53	36
Nashville	8	54	20	1	55	43	2	0	0	30	70	35	11	60	40
New Orleans	23		19	4	68	26	4	1	1	25	39			90	75
Norfolk	58	31	11	0	89	9.6	1.9	0.3	0.2	0.01	0.01	7.4	0.03	74	67
Philadelphia	61	28	11	0	82	10	4.9	0.2	0	15	35	7.8	7.4	88	71
Phoenix	30	60	5	5	15	51	26	1	8	20	20	30	24	70	80
Portland, Oregon	41	33	14	12	21	56	18	2	3	20	53	30	20	82	60
Providence	83	12	5	0	23	55	16	1	1	15	25	35	1.4	21	29
Salt Lake City	7	87	5.5	0	13	69	13	1	3.5	15	20	45	19	56	59
San Antonio	21	59	17	3	28	25	40	1	6	29	31	50	32	46	54
San Diego	10	70	15	5	20	55	25	0.02	0.01	50	70	9	30	80	66
Seattle	38	47	14	1	31	38	11	2	6	25	34	29	14	26	25
St. Louis	61	19	19	1	89	11	0	0	0	12	16	33	0	56	83
St. Paul	37	56	7	0	57	29	10	2	3	4	7	29	0	95	65
Trenton	82	11	6	1	85	6	8	1	0	10	20	65	3	87	62

SOURCE: "Composition of the Homeless Population," in *A Status Report on Hunger and Homelessness in America's Cities, 2000: A 25-City Survey, December 2000*, The United States Conference of Mayors, Washington, DC the constructs of their homeless life (i.e., frequent moves and no school attendance). (See Table 2.5.)

Unaccompanied youth present a special problem to those who wish to study or help the homeless. Many are runaways who avoid contact with adults so as not to be sent back to their homes or placed in foster care. They are "invisible homeless," living on the streets without help from any formal organization or agencies, blending in by day, hiding by night. This is not to ignore the fact, however, that no small number of unaccompanied youth were abandoned or even forced out of their homes by their parents. In 1998 the U.S. Conference of Mayors reported that 3 percent of the homeless it surveyed were unaccompanied youth. In 2000 that number rose to 7 percent. The Urban Institute's 1996 study shows that unaccompanied youth arc much less likely to be served by homeless assistance programs than other homeless people. (See Figure 2.4.)

Homeless children have long been an issue of particular concern to society. Many of the earliest efforts to relieve homelessness were directed toward children, and special efforts continue to be made to prevent child homelessness or, at the very least, to limit its effects. This arises out of a sense that children deserve the best chance society can provide for them and that experiencing homelessness as a child can have serious consequences later in life. Another reason people are increasingly interested in homeless children is because they are more likely to become homeless adults. The 1996 Urban Institute study

found that 21 percent of the homeless adults surveyed had been homeless themselves before the age of 18. (See Figure 2.5.) Also of note is that 33 percent reported having run away from home as a child; 27 percent had been in

FIGURE 2.3

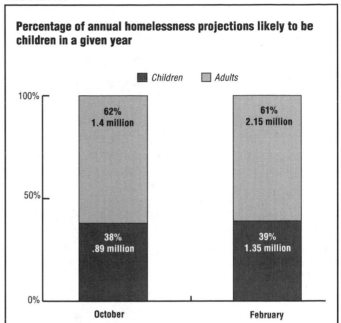

SOURCE: "Percentage of Annual Projections Likely to Be Children in a Given Year," in *America's Homeless II: Populations and Services: National Survey of Homeless Assistance*, Urban Institute, Washington, DC, February 1, 2000

FIGURE 2.4

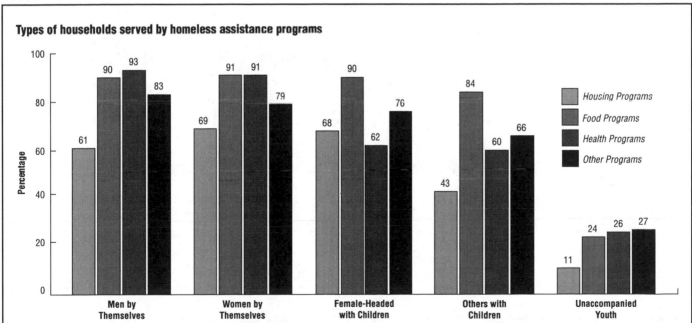

Note: Housing programs include emergency, transitional, permanent housing, and voucher programs; food programs include pantries, soup kitchens, and mobile food programs; health programs include general health, mental health, alcohol/drug, and HIV/AIDS programs; other programs include outreach, drop-in centers, financial/housing assistance, and other.

SOURCE: "Figure 4.8: Types of Households Served by Homeless Assistance Programs," in *Homelessness: Programs and the People They Serve: Findings of the National Survey of Homeless Assistance Providers and Clients*, Urban Institute, Washington, DC, December 1999

TABLE 2.5

Total number of homeless children and youth by grade level

State	K-5 Homeless children and youth	6th-8th Homeless children and youth	9th-12th Homeless children and youth	Total
Alabama	642	4572	1832	7046
Alaska	184	229	944	1357
Arizona[1]	-	-	-	-
Arkansas	4222	1424	2230	7876
California	65591	20633	48029	134253
Colorado	2623	837	883	4343
Connecticut	1753	1106	426	3285
Delaware	663	285	74	1022
Florida	12683	5372	10906	28961
Georgia	3974	2332	3563	9869
Hawaii	579	198	156	933
Idaho[2]	-	-	-	-
Illinois	5679	2583	2188	10450
Indiana[3]	9990	4050	2700	16740
Iowa	2224	2664	3586	8474
Kansas	1063	1194	856	3113
Kentucky	5454	857	959	7270
Louisiana	9504	2227	1905	13636
Maine	446	289	2145	2880
Maryland[4]	4906	-	-	4906
Massachusetts	940	649	1342	2931
Michigan	13800	8700	13000	35500
Minnesota	686	160	164	1010
Mississippi	2697	1276	991	4964
Missouri	3608	1295	1820	6723
Montana	705	499	1164	2368
Nebraska	2310	1108	834	4252
Nevada	1059	233	322	1614
New Hampshire	278	68	74	420
New Jersey	3151	1140	1656	5947
New Mexico	1266	752	2281	4299
New York	12711	7880	3813	24404
North Carolina[5]	1500	800	1500	3800
North Dakota	79	41	21	141
Ohio	11378	5593	5559	22530
Oklahoma	3545	1619	1315	6479
Oregon	6237	3105	2349	11691
Pennsylvania	8204	3004	1785	12993
Puerto Rico	4124	1399	883	6406
Rhode Island	472	315	327	1114
South Carolina	1817	1197	756	3770
South Dakota	2064	1354	838	4256
Tennessee	3158	1895	821	5874
Texas	80136	32548	16908	129592
Utah	6897	3643	3093	13633
Vermont	348	79	220	647
Virginia	4711	1913	1270	7894
Washington[6]	-	-	-	22203
West Virginia	2004	1034	1068	4106
Wisconsin	7034	4858	2211	14103
Wyoming[7]	-	-	-	-
Totals	319099	139009	151767	625330

[1] No report was submitted.
[2] No report was submitted.
[3] State did not collect data regarding enrollment and attendance.
[4] Data reported from shelters, LEAS, and by phone surveys of non-respondents.
[5] This data was derived from 50% of the counties that reported.
[6] Washington reported numbers based on age: 0-5 years: 8048; 6-11 years: 5602; 12-17 years: 4634; and 18-21 years: 3919; Total: 22203
[7] No report was submitted.

SOURCE: "Table 1: Total Number of Homeless Children and Youth by Grade Level," in *Education for Homeless Children and Youth Program: Report to Congress, Fiscal Year 1997*, United States Department of Education, Washington, DC, 1997

foster care or otherwise placed out of the home; and 22 percent had been kicked out of their home before the age of 18. They did not necessarily consider all of these events to have been episodes of homelessness.

In the 1998 edition of its annual study, the AGRM studied the history of the heads of homeless families.

They found that 51 percent of homeless heads of families had not been raised in intact families (families with two parents raising the children together), and 30 percent never had a father at home. Eighteen percent had spent time in foster homes, compared with 27 percent of all homeless adults in the Urban Institute study. Clearly, many children with a background of homelessness or of "broken homes" became the head of a "broken home" themselves. Once again it is important to remember that at least part of the explanation for this trend is poverty. People raised in families with only one parent, or in foster care, are more likely to be poor, precisely because their parents were also more likely to be poor. This poverty makes them more vulnerable to homelessness later in life.

Race and Ethnicity

The major studies differ somewhat when it comes to the exact racial and ethnic makeup of the homeless population. However, they agree that African Americans represent a very large percentage of the homeless population—as large or larger than any other single racial or ethnic group. This is despite findings by the 2000 U.S. Census that African Americans made up only 12.3 percent of the U.S. population, making them the third-largest racial or ethnic group in the country, after whites (75 percent) and Hispanics (12.5 percent). While the studies disagree significantly over what percentage of the homeless are Native American, they do seem to indicate that Native Americans are at least a slightly larger part of the homeless population than they are of the general population, of which they make up only 0.9 percent. Hispanics seem to be the only group that is represented in both the general and homeless populations in roughly the same proportions. Even according to the highest estimates, whites and Asian Americans make up much smaller percentages of the homeless population than they do the general population.

It is clear from these statistics that African Americans are particularly likely to become homeless. No one can say the exact reason why this is so, but as always, poverty is definitely a major reason. On average, African Americans do not earn as much money as whites or Asian Americans. However, while the same can be said of Hispanics, their percentage of the homeless population is much smaller than that of African Americans, so other factors must be involved.

Veterans

Veterans are a part of the homeless population that has been subject to special attention, as veterans are entitled to government benefits and have strong advocacy groups of their own. Nevertheless, it is unclear exactly how many homeless people have served in the military. In 1996 the Urban Institute found that 23 percent of homeless people were veterans, compared with 13 percent of the overall population. (See Table 1.3 in Chapter 1.) However this was due in part to the fact that more men were homeless than women, and almost all veterans were men. In 1996 the percentage of homeless men who were veterans was 33 percent, compared with 31 percent of all American men. The AGRM's 1999 study found that 30

FIGURE 2.5

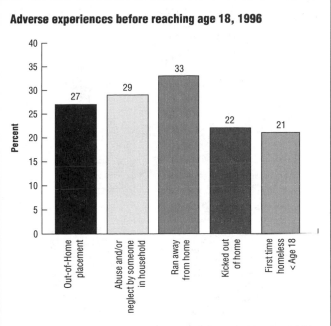

Adverse experiences before reaching age 18, 1996

SOURCE: "Figure 2.12: Adverse Experiences before Reaching Age 18," in *Homelessness: Programs and the People They Serve: Findings of the National Survey of Homeless Assistance Providers and Clients,* Urban Institute, Washington, DC, December 1999

percent of homeless people were veterans. In 2000, however, the U.S. Conference of Mayors found that 15 percent of the homeless population were veterans. Based on these conflicting reports, it is impossible to say exactly how many homeless people are veterans, but it is clearly a significant number.

The National Coalition for Homeless Veterans, a veterans advocacy group, reports that veterans are more likely to cite substance abuse as being largely responsible for their living conditions than the typical homeless person. Homeless veterans are also more likely to be white, better educated, and more likely to have been married than homeless nonveterans, according to the group. Minorities are overrepresented among homeless veterans, just as they are in the homeless population in general. About two out of five homeless veterans are African American or Hispanic. However, there is some evidence that veteran status reduces vulnerability to homelessness among blacks, most likely because of the educational and other benefits to which veterans are entitled.

The Elderly

Very little research has been done on the elderly homeless, who make up only a small proportion of the homeless. The Urban Institute study (see Table 1.3 in Chapter 1) reports a 2 percent elderly homeless population, and the AGRM study (see Table 1.2 in Chapter 1) reports 5 percent. There are three main theories as to why there are relatively few elderly homeless:

FIGURE 2.6

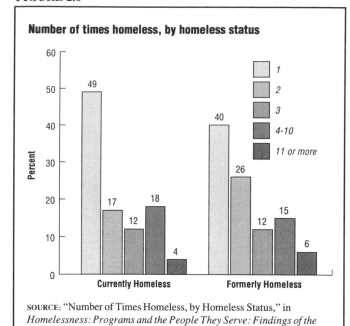

Number of times homeless, by homeless status

SOURCE: "Number of Times Homeless, by Homeless Status," in *Homelessness: Programs and the People They Serve: Findings of the National Survey of Homeless Assistance Providers and Clients,* Urban Institute, Washington, DC, December 1999

- After age 65, many who have been homeless become entitled to benefits such as Social Security, Medicare, and special housing, enabling them to get enough help and income to become housed.

- Many homeless do not live long enough to become elderly; they come to the streets in poor health, and the hardships of being homeless shorten their lives.

- Survey methods: The elderly do not frequent places they fear are dangerous, such as some shelters and other programs where interviews take place. Therefore, they may not receive adequate representation by sampling techniques used in some surveys.

Education

Results from the 1996 Urban Institute study show that more than half of the homeless in the survey completed high school or achieved a GED. (See Table 1.3 in Chapter 1.) Of those, 28 percent had education beyond high school. Thirty-eight percent of homeless clients had dropped out of high school. Homeless people are less educated than the general adult U.S. population: only 25 percent of American adults (those ages 25 and older) had less than a high school education; 34 percent had a high school diploma; and 45 percent had some education beyond high school. The adult members of homeless families are even less likely to have a full education than single homeless people. Those who have not completed high school make up 53 percent of this group, and 36 percent have no more than a high school education. However, they are just as likely as unattached homeless people to have some schooling beyond high school.

REOCCURANCE AND DURATION OF HOMELESSNESS

Homelessness is generally not a brief situation caused by a temporary emergency. The majority of homeless nationally are not homeless for the first time. Homeless spells for the majority last less than one year. The AGRM study (see Table 1.2 in Chapter 1) found that 69 percent of people remained homeless less than one year in the surveyed cities. It also found that only 33 percent were homeless for the first time, with 29 percent homeless for the second time, and 20 percent having been homeless three or more times.

In the 1996 Urban Institute study, currently and formerly homeless clients were asked about their experiences with homelessness, including how many times they had been homeless, the length of their current homeless episode (if homeless at the time of the survey), and the length of the most recent, completed episode of homelessness (for formerly homeless clients and currently homeless clients who had been homeless more than once).

According to the study, currently homeless clients were more likely than formerly homeless clients to have had only one homeless episode (49 percent versus 40 percent). (See Figure 2.6.) Similar proportions of currently and formerly homeless clients (22 and 21 percent, respectively) had been homeless four or more times. Twenty-eight percent of currently homeless clients had been homeless during their present spell for three months or less, while 30 percent had been homeless for two years or more. The most frequently mentioned spell length was between one and three months (33 and 30 percent, respectively). The next most frequently mentioned category was episodes of 7–12 months, indicated by 21 and 20 percent, respectively. Relatively few clients reported episodes of two years or more.

THE RURAL HOMELESS

The vast majority of studies on the homeless have been limited to those in urban areas, leading many to believe the problem exists only on city sidewalks. It is true that homelessness is more common in the cities, in part because housing is more expensive. However, many areas of rural America are also struggling with homelessness. Rural communities have fewer official shelters and fewer public places, such as heating grates and subway or train stations, at which the homeless can congregate. This makes the rural homeless even harder to count and provide help to than the urban homeless.

In 1996 the U.S. Department of Agriculture (USDA), in *Rural Homelessness: Focusing on the Needs of the Rural Homeless,* reported that homeless people in rural areas were more likely to be white, female, married, and currently working than the urban homeless. They were

FIGURE 2.7

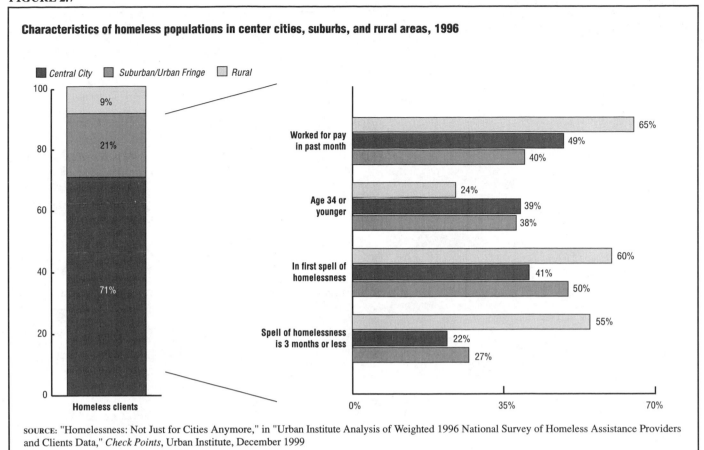

Characteristics of homeless populations in center cities, suburbs, and rural areas, 1996

■ *Central City* ■ *Suburban/Urban Fringe* □ *Rural*

SOURCE: "Homelessness: Not Just for Cities Anymore," in "Urban Institute Analysis of Weighted 1996 National Survey of Homeless Assistance Providers and Clients Data," *Check Points*, Urban Institute, December 1999

also more likely to be homeless for the first time and generally had experienced homelessness for a shorter period of time than the urban homeless. Findings also included higher rates of domestic violence and lower rates of alcohol and substance abuse.

The Urban Institute study, *Homelessness: Programs and the People They Serve,* determined that 21 percent of all homeless people in their study lived in suburban areas, and 9 percent lived in rural communities. (See Figure 2.7.) This study agrees with the USDA's study in many areas. The rural homeless it surveyed were more likely to be working, or have worked recently, than the urban homeless—65 percent of the rural homeless had worked for pay in the last month. Homeless people living in rural areas were also more likely to be experiencing their first spell of homelessness (60 percent). In 55 percent of the cases, the homeless spell lasted three months or less.

The rural homeless are often hidden and do not receive the same amount of attention their urban counterparts receive. Although housing costs are generally lower in rural areas than in cities, rural incomes are also lower.

The rural homeless may live in shacks rather than shelters or may be taken in by family members. They can be found in cars, abandoned buildings, and even in the woods, when nothing else is available. The rural homeless are also less likely to get social services and benefits than they would in the cities because rural areas generally lack the social support services found in more urban areas.

Several types of rural areas generate higher-than-average levels of homelessness, including regions that:

• Are primarily agricultural—residents often lose their livelihood because of reduced demand for farm labor or because of a shrinking service sector.

• Depend on declining extractive industries, such as mining or timber.

• Are experiencing economic growth—new or expanding industrial plants often attract more job seekers than can be absorbed.

• Have persistent poverty, such as Appalachia, where the young and able-bodied may have to relocate before they can find work.

CHAPTER 3

EMPLOYMENT AND POVERTY AMONG THE HOMELESS

POVERTY AND HOMELESSNESS

Poverty does not necessarily mean homelessness; most of the nation's poor are not homeless. The homeless, however, are poor, and those living at or below the poverty level are often teetering on the edge of homelessness. Poverty, as it is commonly understood, means not having enough money for the necessities of life. Difficult choices must be made when limited resources cover only some of the necessities. It can mean going hungry, living in substandard conditions or on the streets, or not going to the doctor when one is sick because there is not enough money to pay the bill. Often it is housing, which absorbs a high proportion of income, that the poor choose to give up—assuming that they are even given the choice. The poor do not generally own real estate; they have to pay rent. If they fall behind on these payments, they become evicted. Since these people were unable to pay their old rent, it is quite likely they will not be able to find new housing that they can afford, and so they become homeless. For many people, homelessness is just a month's rent away. Even those who do own a home are likely to have a mortgage, with payments that must be met or else their house will be taken by the bank.

Homelessness, then, is overwhelmingly linked to poverty. It is impossible to understand homelessness without understanding poverty.

MEASURING POVERTY

The Official Poverty Threshold

The federal government defines poverty as specific levels of income for individuals and families, excluding noncash benefits (such as food stamps, Medicaid, or subsidized housing), taxes owed, or tax deductions. The poverty index was developed during the 1960s based upon the Department of Agriculture's 1955 Household Food Consumption Survey, which had determined that a family

TABLE 3.1

Preliminary estimate of weighted average poverty thresholds for 2000

Size of Family Unit	Estimated Threshold
1 person (unrelated individual)	$8,787
Under 65 years	$8,958
65 years and over	$8,259
2 people	$11,234
Householder under 65 years	$11,591
Householder 65 years and over	$10,414
3 people	$13,737
4 people	$17,601
5 people	$20,804
6 people	$23,491
7 people	$26,783
8 people	$29,941
9 people or more	$35,574

Note: These average poverty thresholds were derived by increasing the 1999 thresholds by a factor of 1.033613 which reflects the percent change in the average annual Consumer Price Index between 1999 and 2000. These estimates may differ by a few dollars from the thresholds published in the final report on the 2000 poverty population.

SOURCE: "Preliminary estimate of weighted average poverty thresholds for 2000," U.S. Census Bureau, Washington, DC, January 24, 2001

of three spent approximately one-third of its income on food. The poverty threshold for a family of three was therefore set at three times the cost of the Economy Food Plan. The government has since revised the poverty threshold regularly to account for inflation and changes in the economy. In 2000 the U.S. Department of Commerce set the poverty threshold for a family of four at $17,601 (up from the 1997 guidelines set by the Social Security Administration of $16,400). (Table 3.1) The thresholds range from $8,259 for an elderly person living alone to $35,574 for a family of nine or more members.

CONCERNS REGARDING THE ACCURACY OF THE POVERTY THRESHOLD. In 2001 The Conveners of the Working Group on Revising the Poverty Measure—a group of economists, lawyers, professors, and social acad-

TABLE 3.2

Comparison of summary measures of income by selected characteristics, 1989, 1998, and 1999

Characteristics	Number (thous.)	1999 Median income		Median income in 1998 (In 1999 dollars)		Median income in 1989r (In 1999 dollars)		Percent change in real income 1998 to 1999		Percent change in real income 1989r to 1999	
		Value (dollars)	90-percent confidence interval (+/-) (dollars)	Value (dollars)	90-percent confidence interval (+/-) (dollars)	Value (dollars)	90-percent confidence interval (+/-) (dollars)	Percent change	90-percent confidence interval (+/-)	Percent change	90-percent confidence interval (+/-)
Households											
All households	104,705	40,816	314	39,744	387	38,721	351	2.7 *	1.0	5.4 *	1.3
Type of Household											
Family households	72,025	49,940	449	48,517	419	46,344	422	2.9 *	1.0	7.8 *	1.4
Married-couple families	55,311	56,827	502	55,475	541	51,822	469	2.4 *	1.1	9.7 *	1.4
Female householder, no husband present	12,687	26,164	594	24,932	669	23,163	617	4.9 *	3.0	13.0 *	4.0
Male householder, no wife present	4,028	41,838	1,311	40,284	1,670	40,594	1,642	3.9	4.4	3.1	5.3
Nonfamily households	32,680	24,566	444	23,959	477	23,066	371	2.5 *	2.2	6.5 *	2.6
Female householder	18,039	19,917	454	19,026	472	18,544	484	4.7 *	2.8	7.4 *	3.7
Male householder	14,641	30,753	568	31,086	572	30,140	674	-1.1	2.1	2.0	3.0
Race and Hispanic Origin of Householder											
All races[1]	104,705	40,816	314	39,744	387	38,721	351	2.7 *	1.0	5.4 *	1.3
White	87,671	42,504	393	41,816	343	40,732	327	1.6 *	1.0	4.3 *	1.3
Non-Hispanic	78,819	44,366	459	43,376	410	41,693	338	2.3 *	1.2	6.4 *	1.4
Black	12,849	27,910	854	25,911	667	24,479	807	7.7 *	3.5	14.0 *	5.1
Asian and Pacific Islander	3,337	51,205	3,088	47,667	2,182	48,383	2,051	7.4 *	6.6	5.8	7.8
Hispanic[2]	9,319	30,735	747	28,956	916	29,264	902	6.1 *	2.9	5.0 *	4.1
Age of Householder											
15 to 24 years	5,860	25,171	689	24,084	748	24,940	771	4.5 *	3.5	0.9	4.2
25 to 34 years	18,627	42,174	661	40,954	711	39,903	617	3.0 *	1.9	5.7 *	2.3
35 to 44 years	23,955	50,873	653	49,521	747	50,399	690	2.7 *	1.6	0.9	1.9
45 to 54 years	20,927	56,917	875	55,344	898	55,780	913	2.8 *	1.9	2.0	2.3
55 to 64 years	13,592	44,597	1,063	44,120	1,010	41,465	897	1.1	2.7	7.6 *	3.5
65 years and over	21,745	22,812	375	22,209	404	21,177	389	2.7 *	2.0	7.7 *	2.7
Nativity of the householder											
Native born	93,062	41,383	336	40,553	398	(NA)	(NA)	2.0 *	1.1	X	X
Foreign born	11,643	36,048	949	33,691	1,258	(NA)	(NA)	7.0 *	4.0	X	X
Naturalized citizen	5,383	43,947	2,418	41,934	1,848	(NA)	(NA)	4.8	6.0	X	X
Not a citizen	6,260	31,199	1,031	28,903	1,226	(NA)	(NA)	7.9 *	4.7	X	X
Region											
Northeast	20,087	41,984	699	41,531	789	43,724	725	1.1	2.5	-4.0 *	2.3
Midwest	24,508	42,679	832	41,506	614	38,517	656	2.8 *	1.8	10.8 *	2.9
South	37,303	37,442	548	36,588	511	34,682	482	2.3 *	2.1	8.0 *	2.2
West	22,808	42,720	783	41,888	678	41,604	712	2.0	2.8	2.7 *	2.6
Residence											
Inside metropolitan areas	84,259	42,785	456	41,888	361	41,677	354	2.1 *	1.1	2.7 *	1.4
Inside central cities	31,825	35,573	505	33,883	652	(NA)	(NA)	5.0 *	2.0	X	X
Outside central cities	52,433	47,708	625	47,427	523	(NA)	(NA)	0.6	1.4	X	X
Outside metropolitan areas	20,447	33,021	931	32,729	644	30,042	650	0.9	2.8	9.9 *	3.7

TABLE 3.2

Comparison of summary measures of income by selected characteristics, 1989, 1998, and 1999

Characteristics	Number (thous.)	1999 Median income		Median income in 1998 (in 1999 dollars)		Median income in 1989r (in 1999 dollars)		Percent change in real income 1998 to 1999		Percent change in real income 1989r to 1999	
		Value (dollars)	90-percent confidence interval (+/-) (dollars)	Value (dollars)	90-percent confidence interval (+/-) (dollars)	Value (dollars)	90-percent confidence interval (+/-) (dollars)	Percent change	90-percent confidence interval (+/-)	Percent change	90-percent confidence interval (+/-)
Earnings of full-time, year-round workers											
Male	57,511	36,476	224	36,126	224	36,516	248	1.0 *	0.7	-0.1	0.9
Female	40,404	26,324	186	26,433	198	25,158	276	-0.4	0.8	4.6 *	1.4
Per Capita Income											
All races[1]	274,087	21,181	206	20,564	206	18,683	132	3.0 *	1.2	13.4 *	1.3
White	224,806	22,375	243	21,867	243	19,813	150	2.3 *	1.3	12.9 *	1.3
Non-Hispanic	193,633	24,109	288	23,459	285	(NA)	(NA)	2.8 *	1.5	X	X
Black	35,509	14,397	383	13,243	334	11,658	247	8.7 *	3.3	23.5 *	3.8
Asian and Pacific Islander	10,925	21,134	1,179	19,122	1,124	(NA)	(NA)	10.5 *	7.5	X	X
Hispanic[2]	32,804	11,621	373	11,687	424	11,008	283	-0.6	3.6	5.6 *	4.1

* Statistically significant change at the 90-percent confidence level.
r Revised to reflect the population distribution reported in the 1990 census.
[1] Data for American Indians and Alaska Natives are not shown separately in this tab e.
[2] Hispanics may be of any race.

SOURCE: "Income 1999: Table A. Comparison of Summary Measures of Income by Selected Characteristics: 1989, 1998, and 1999," in *Current Population Survey*, U.S. Census Bureau, Washington, DC, March 1990, 1999, and 2000

FIGURE 3.1

Number of poor and poverty rate, 1959 to 1999

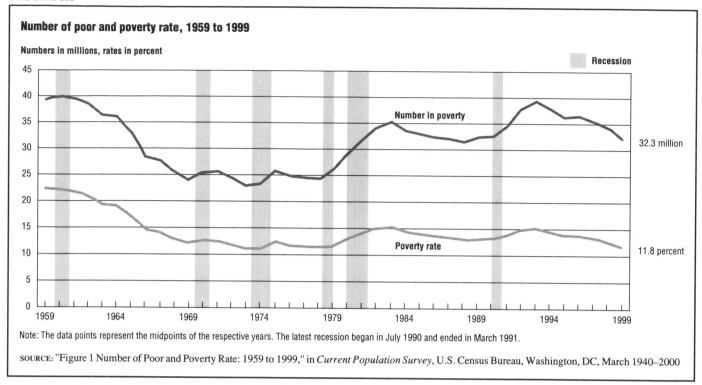

Note: The data points represent the midpoints of the respective years. The latest recession began in July 1990 and ended in March 1991.

SOURCE: "Figure 1 Number of Poor and Poverty Rate: 1959 to 1999," in *Current Population Survey*, U.S. Census Bureau, Washington, DC, March 1940–2000

emics—wrote *"An Open Letter on Revising the Official Measure of Poverty"* to the Director of the Office of Management and Budget. They wrote to express their concerns over the inadequacy of the current official poverty level measurement and to propose a set of guidelines for a revised standard. The letter states that the current system is one that was established in 1960, at a time when the dollar went much further than today. These people and others have criticized the government's version of poverty for years, claiming that it's deceptive: it fails to recognize true poverty. In that light, it is important to consider that the current poverty statistics may be underrepresenting a large percentage of truly impoverished people.

Median Income

The 1999 median household income as shown in Table 3.2, for all households in the United States (may be unrelated individuals) was $40,816. Not surprisingly, median family income varied greatly according to family composition. The median income for married-couple families was $56,827, but for female-headed families with no husband present, it was only $26,164, less than half that of a couple-headed family. Race was also a factor. In 1997 Asian and Pacific Islander households had the highest median income ($51,205). The median income for white households was $42,504; for Hispanics, $30,735; and for blacks, $27,910.

Considering that the median income lies in the middle of what all people in a particular group earn, it is clear from these statistics that large numbers of families headed

by single women, Hispanics, or African Americans, must be at or below the poverty level. These groups earn less money at their jobs than white men earn at theirs.

The Official Poverty Rate

The percent or the U.S. population earning wages below the poverty threshold or level is generally known as the poverty rate. As part of its Current Population Survey (CPS), the U.S. Census Bureau attempts to measure the poverty rate on an ongoing basis. The CPS reported that in 1999, 32.3 million people lived below the official government poverty level, a poverty rate of 11.8 percent, down from the 12.7 percent poverty rate in 1998 (*Poverty 1999, U.S. Census Bureau, Current Population Survey,* March 1940–2000). Figure 3.1 shows how both the total number of poor and the poverty rate have fluctuated since the 1970s.

Evaluating Poverty from a Local Level

In 2000 elected municipal officials of U.S. cities rated the issues that had improved or worsened in their cities that year. The 2000 National League of Cities results showed that 9 percent of the cities reported that poverty had worsened in their municipalities in the past year. In 18 percent of the cities, officials said poverty had lessened, and 73 percent reported no change. Fifty percent of those same officials reported that employment had increased, while only 6 percent said it had worsened, leaving 44 percent who responded that there had been no change in their cities. (See Figure 2.1, Chapter 2.) However, it is important to note that this survey is not a scientific study of

TABLE 3.3

Share of aggregate income received by each fifth and top five percent of families, 1947–99

	Lowest fifth	Second fifth	Middle fifth	Fourth fifth	Highest fifth	Top 5 percent
1947	5.0	11.9	17.0	23.1	43.0	17.5
1948	4.9	12.1	17.3	23.2	42.4	17.1
1949	4.5	11.9	17.3	23.5	42.7	16.9
1950	4.5	12.0	17.4	23.4	42.7	17.3
1951	5.0	12.4	17.6	23.4	41.6	16.8
1952	4.9	12.3	17.4	23.4	41.9	17.4
1953	4.7	12.5	18.0	23.9	40.9	15.7
1954	4.5	12.1	17.7	23.9	41.8	16.3
1955	4.8	12.3	17.8	23.7	41.3	16.4
1956	5.0	12.5	17.9	23.7	41.0	16.1
1957	5.1	12.7	18.1	23.8	40.4	15.6
1958	5.0	12.5	18.0	23.9	40.6	15.4
1959	4.9	12.3	17.9	23.8	41.1	15.9
1960	4.8	12.2	17.8	24.0	41.3	15.9
1961	4.7	11.9	17.5	23.8	42.2	16.6
1962	5.0	12.1	17.6	24.0	41.3	15.7
1963	5.0	12.1	17.7	24.0	41.2	15.8
1964	5.1	12.0	17.7	24.0	41.2	15.9
1965	5.2	12.2	17.8	23.9	40.9	15.5
1966	5.6	12.4	17.8	23.8	40.5	15.6
1967	5.4	12.2	17.5	23.5	41.4	16.4
1968	5.6	12.4	17.7	23.7	40.5	15.6
1969	5.6	12.4	17.7	23.7	40.6	15.6
1970	5.4	12.2	17.6	23.8	40.9	15.6
1971	5.5	12.0	17.6	23.8	41.1	15.7
1972	5.5	11.9	17.5	23.9	41.4	15.9
1973	5.5	11.9	17.5	24.0	41.1	15.5
1974	5.7	12.0	17.6	24.1	40.6	14.8
1975	5.6	11.9	17.7	24.2	40.7	14.9
1976	5.6	11.9	17.7	24.2	40.7	14.9
1977	5.5	11.7	17.6	24.3	40.9	14.9
1978	5.4	11.7	17.6	24.2	41.1	15.1
1979	5.4	11.6	17.5	24.1	41.4	15.3
1980	5.3	11.6	17.6	24.4	41.1	14.6
1981	5.3	11.4	17.5	24.6	41.2	14.4
1982	5.0	11.3	17.2	24.4	42.2	15.3
1983	4.9	11.2	17.2	24.5	42.4	15.3
1984	4.8	11.1	17.1	24.5	42.5	15.4
1985	4.8	11.0	16.9	24.3	43.1	16.1
1986	4.7	10.9	16.9	24.1	43.4	16.5
1987	4.6	10.7	16.8	24.0	43.8	17.2
1988	4.6	10.7	16.7	24.0	44.0	17.2
1989	4.6	10.6	16.5	23.7	44.6	17.9
1990	4.6	10.8	16.6	23.8	44.3	17.4
1991	4.5	10.7	16.6	24.1	44.2	17.1
1992	4.3	10.5	16.5	24.0	44.7	17.6
1993	4.1	9.9	15.7	23.3	47.0	20.3
1994	4.2	10.0	15.7	23.3	46.9	20.1
1995	4.4	10.1	15.8	23.2	46.5	20.0
1996	4.2	10.0	15.8	23.1	46.8	20.3
1997	4.2	9.9	15.7	23	47.2	20.7
1998	4.2	9.9	15.7	23	47.3	20.7
1999	4.3	9.9	15.6	23	47.2	20.3

Note: It appears that between the years 1974 and 1986 negative amounts were included in the aggregate.
These data were revised to maintain comparability with the majority of years where negative amounts were treated as zeros.

SOURCE: "Share of aggregate income received by each fifth and top 5 percent of families, 1947–99," in "National Data, Wage and Compensation Trends," *The State of Working America 2000–01*, Economic Policy Institute, Washington, DC, May 2001

whether poverty is itself increasing or decreasing, but rather an informal poll of how concerned city officials across the United States are about poverty.

Trends in the Poverty Rate

For the most part, the poverty rate is linked to the performance of the U.S. economy. When the economy is in recession, the poverty rate increases. Actually, the poverty rate often begins to increase somewhat before a serious economic downturn, and may not begin to decline until some time after a recession ends.

Figure 3.1 demonstrates that during the recession of 1980–82, when many Americans lost their jobs and the economy performed poorly, the poverty rate increased dramatically. In 1979, the year before the recession began, the poverty rate was 11.7 percent; by 1983 it stood at 15.2 percent. After the recession of the early 1980s ended, the

FIGURE 3.2

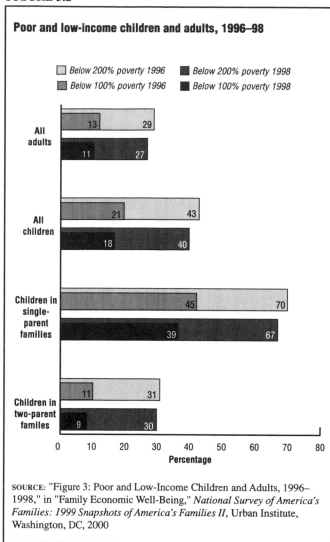

Poor and low-income children and adults, 1996–98

Legend:
☐ Below 200% poverty 1996   ■ Below 200% poverty 1998
▨ Below 100% poverty 1996   ■ Below 100% poverty 1998

All adults: 13, 29, 11, 27

All children: 21, 43, 18, 40

Children in single-parent families: 45, 70, 39, 67

Children in two-parent families: 11, 31, 9, 30

Percentage (0 10 20 30 40 50 60 70 80)

SOURCE: "Figure 3: Poor and Low-Income Children and Adults, 1996–1998," in "Family Economic Well-Being," *National Survey of America's Families: 1999 Snapshots of America's Families II*, Urban Institute, Washington, DC, 2000

increase in births, which happened in the 1980s and 1990s, as these same latter-day baby boomers became adults and parents. Since wealth begets wealthy children and poverty begets poor children, the proportion of people living in poverty grew because 1) more of these parents were working in low-wage jobs than others had in earlier years, thus birthing their children into poverty and 2) the addition of children dropped families who had been above the poverty level, down into it. For example, Table 3.1 shows the year 2000 poverty threshold for a family of three at $13, 737. If a family of three made $15,000 per year, then that family was above below the federal definition of the poverty level. But if another child was born in that family, they would then fall into the poverty level figures because a family of four needs $17,601 a year to stay out of poverty. The total poverty numbers have now been increased by the addition of four more people.

Poverty Rates in the New Millennium

In 1999 the United States had its lowest poverty rate, 11.8 percent, since 1979 (Figure 3.1). The Center on Budget and Policy Priorities reports that while census data show that the number of poor Americans has fallen markedly in recent years, those who remain poor have grown poorer. Using a measure of poverty that accounts for all money directly received into the household such as noncash benefits, the Earned Income Tax Credit, and subtracting income and payroll taxes, the average poor person fell farther below the poverty line in 1999 than in any year since 1979. When the poor become significantly poorer, increased homelessness is the result. The most recent poverty and homeless figures, compared to the official economic outlook, support this contention.

THE DISTRIBUTION OF WEALTH

While most discussions of poverty focus simply on people who are below the poverty line versus those who are above it, it is important to keep in mind that even among the poor, there are those who are worse off than others. The distribution of wealth and poverty among the population as a whole is a major factor in homelessness. The distribution of wealth also helps to explain why homelessness and poverty can increase or remain level, even when the economy performs well.

Many people became poor in the 1980s and early 1990s at the same time that many others became very wealthy. Table 3.3 breaks the U.S. population down into five groups based on income, ranging from the fifth of the population with the lowest incomes to the fifth with the highest incomes. It then displays what percent of all income each fifth of the population made in each year, as well as the amount of wealth possessed by those whose income was in the top five percent of all Americans (the highest fifth of the highest fifth).

poverty rate gradually declined. By 1989 it was down to 12.8 percent, its lowest level since 1979. The United States then endured another recession in 1990–91, and by its end the poverty level was up to 14.2 percent.

Forces Behind Changes in the Poverty Rate

POVERTY RATES INCREASE IN A LOW-WAGE LABOR MARKET. Increases in these numbers can occur when there is a large increase in people entering the labor force, such as in 1980 when the last cohorts of the baby boom generation (those born between 1947 and 1961) began to reach working age. Because the 1970s and 1980s saw significant middle-income job losses, as factories moved to countries where workers could be paid much less, a larger percentage of available entry-level positions in the 1980s and 1990s were in the low-paying service industry. Those entering the job market were poorly paid, and this increased the numbers living in poverty.

BIRTHS CREATE INCREASED POVERTY. Another factor that can affect the growing numbers in poverty is an

FIGURE 3.3

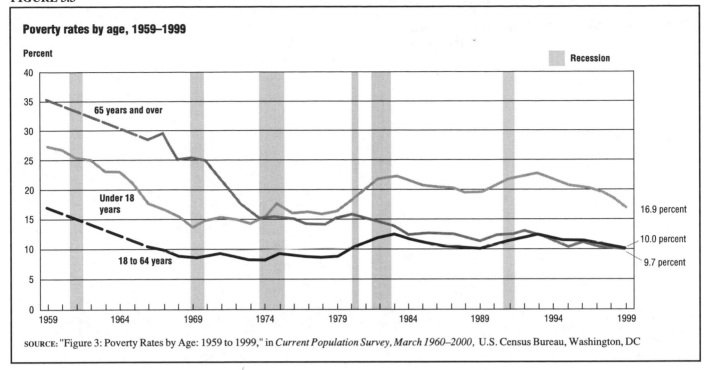

Poverty rates by age, 1959–1999

SOURCE: "Figure 3: Poverty Rates by Age: 1959 to 1999," in *Current Population Survey, March 1960–2000*, U.S. Census Bureau, Washington, DC

From 1991 to 1999, the highest fifth increased their income from 44.2 percent of the total to 47.2 percent. Every other fifth of the population saw their percentage of income decline. The lowest fifth went from 4.5 percent of all income in 1991 down to 4.1 percent in 1993, only to recover slightly and return to 4.3 percent by 1999. The top five percent of Americans saw their percentage of all income increase from 17.1 percent to 20.3 percent. What all of this means is that even though the U.S. economy went through a period of historic growth during the 1990s, most of the new wealth generated by this growth went into the hands of those who were already relatively wealthy. The poor, if anything, became even poorer. Historically, the growth in the gap between the rich and the poor indicates (or leads to) increased homelessness.

WHO ARE THE POOR?

Each year, the Urban Institute publishes a "snapshot" report on American families, The National Survey of America's Families (NSAF). (*National Survey of America's Families 1999 Snapshots of America's Families II Family Economic Well-Being,* Urban Institute, 2000.) The 1999 report reveals that generally speaking, American families were better off financially in 1998 than in 1997. The poverty rate for nonelderly adults (those below 65 years of age) declined from about 13 percent in 1997 to 11 percent in 1998.

The percentage of adults with low incomes (incomes of no more than twice the poverty level) also declined slightly, from 29 percent in 1996 to 27 percent in 1998. The percentage of nonelderly adults classified as low income in 1998

varied significantly across the states. Rates ranged from a low of about 18 percent in Massachusetts, Minnesota, and New Jersey to a high of 38 percent in Texas.

Reductions in poverty from previous years were strong for children. The percentage of children classified as poor declined from 21 percent in 1996 to 18 percent in 1998. But still they are society's poorest members (Figure 3.2). The poverty rate for all children in 1998 was nearly two-thirds more than that for nonelderly adults: 18 percent, compared with 11 percent. Children living in single-parent families experienced the largest decline in their poverty rate, from almost 45 percent in 1996 to 39 percent in 1998. This is consistent with an employment increase for single-parent families.

For a number of years, poverty has steadily decreased for people 65 and over and risen for children under 18. Figure 3.3 from the 1999 Census Bureau CPS (Current Population Survey) shows the patterns of poverty since 1959 through 1999.

An Urban Institute study of federal funding for children shows a correlation between the amount of federal social program funding and poverty rates. (*Federal Expenditures on Children: 1960–1997,* Clark, King, Spiro, Steuerle, Urban Institute, 2001.) Simply put, when the numbers in Figure 3.4 are compared with those in Figure 3.3, it shows that as government spending for children increased, poverty among children decreased. Note in Figure 3.4 the increasing rate of children's spending following the year 1995 compared to the decreasing poverty rate for children in Figure 3.3 for the same year. The government

FIGURE 3.4

Federal expenditures on children and other major items, 1960–97

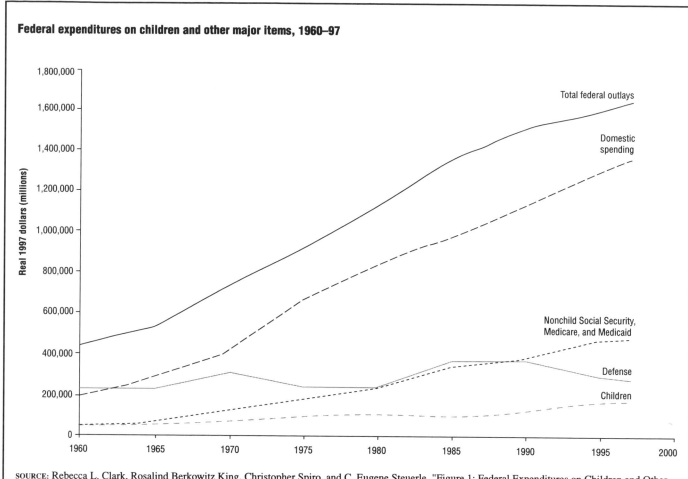

SOURCE: Rebecca L. Clark, Rosalind Berkowitz King, Christopher Spiro, and C. Eugene Steuerle, "Figure 1: Federal Expenditures on Children and Other Major Items," in *Federal Expenditures on Children: 1960–1997*, Urban Institute, Washington, DC, April 2001

spending/poverty rate connection is also demonstrated by federal funding towards the elderly in Figure 3.4. The spending for elderly programs (Nonchild Social Security, Medicare, and Medicaid) has shot up at a far quicker rate than that to benefit children. The rapid decrease in the poverty rate for 65 years of age and older is widely attributed to this government spending (Figure 3.3).

Children

Taken as a group, the poorest members of U.S. society are children, especially the children of single mothers. According to the results from the 1999 NSAF study, children living in single parent families had the highest percentage of poverty at almost 67 percent, more than twice the 30 percent rate for children living with two parents (Figure 3.2). The percentage of children living in low-income families declined from 43 percent in 1996 to 40 percent in 1998.

Single Mothers

Single mothers are the next largest group of people below the poverty line after children. Even single mothers

who work are likely to be poor. The 1999 CPS reveals that the highest poverty rate among family heads is that of female householder families with no worker (67.9 percent), and female-headed families where the woman worked were still far more likely, at 24.4 percent, to be in poverty than married-couple families (Figure 3.5).

Race and Ethnicity

Hispanics and African Americans are much more likely to be poor than members of other racial and ethnic groups. The 1999 CPS found that the poverty rate for Hispanics (who may be of any race) declined from 25.6 percent in 1998 to 22.8 percent in 1999. The poverty rate for African Americans was at a record low in 1999 of 23.6 percent, down from the previous low of 26.1 percent in 1998. Nevertheless, this was much higher than the poverty rate of 7.7 percent for whites and 10.7 percent for Asian Americans and Pacific Islanders.

Poverty Trends by Region

The poverty rate varies significantly from one part of the United States to another. The 1999 CPS showed a

FIGURE 3.5

FIGURE 3.6

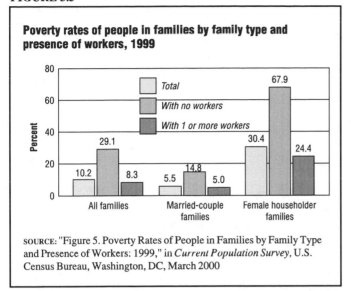

Poverty rates of people in families by family type and presence of workers, 1999

SOURCE: "Figure 5. Poverty Rates of People in Families by Family Type and Presence of Workers: 1999," in *Current Population Survey*, U.S. Census Bureau, Washington, DC, March 2000

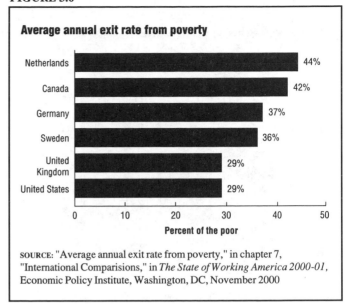

Average annual exit rate from poverty

SOURCE: "Average annual exit rate from poverty," in chapter 7, "International Comparisions," in *The State of Working America 2000-01*, Economic Policy Institute, Washington, DC, November 2000

decline in the poverty rate from 1998 numbers in the Northeast and West, dropping from 12.3 percent and 14.0 percent to 10.9 percent and 12.6 percent, respectively. The poverty rate did not change significantly for those in the South or Midwest. Four-fifths (81 percent) of the total decline in the number of poor occurred in central cities, despite the fact that only 29 percent of all people and 41 percent of the poor lived there.

In seven states and in the District of Columbia, the poverty rate decreased significantly, based on comparing two-year moving averages of 1998–99 with those for 1997–98. These states were Arizona, Arkansas, California, the District of Columbia, New York, South Dakota, Utah, and Virginia. No state showed an increase.

The 1999 National Survey of America's Families study reports that children in poverty is a problem for the nation as a whole, but for some states it has reached distressing proportions. More than one in five children in Alabama, California, Mississippi, New York, and Texas live in poverty.

EXITING POVERTY

Poverty is not a static condition. Even when the poverty level stays roughly the same for long periods, a great number of people are becoming poor for the first time each year, while some poor people are able to improve their economic footing and move out of poverty. Unfortunately, while the CPS presents annual poverty data, these surveys do not reflect the dynamic nature of poverty for individual persons and families. There is little national data available on exiting or entering poverty. An older study from The Bureau of the Census in 1992 provides a reasonable picture. (The Bureau of the Census, *Dynamics of Economic Well-Being: Poverty, 1992 to 1993*, Washington, DC, 1995.) This study found that:

• Among the chronically poor, blacks and people in female-headed households were most likely to remain poor.

• Unemployment was the primary reason for poverty for the largest percentage of those who were poor for more than two months.

• Among those who exited poverty, married-couple families, whites, and persons 18 to 64 years of age were most likely to do so.

Comparisons from the Economic Policy Institute show that exiting poverty is harder in the United States than in other countries (Figure 3.6). In the year 2000 the United States fell at the bottom of the list of fellow industrialized nations in terms of people's ability to remove themselves from poverty. On average, about 28.6 percent of the poor in the United States escape poverty each year. The share of the poor leaving poverty in the other countries ranges from 29.1 percent in the United Kingdom to 43.7 percent in the Netherlands. The poor in the United States are also more likely than the poor in other countries to fall back into poverty once they make it out. (Economic Policy Institute, *The State of Working America 2000–01, International Comparisons,* Oxley, Dang, and Antolin, November 2000.)

EMPLOYMENT AND INCOME TRENDS

History has demonstrated that the lack of jobs leads to homelessness for those at the far edge of poverty. When the disparity of wealth between the rich and the poor grows too wide, it indicates job losses or below-subsistence wages for the bottom 20 percent of society. Those at the very bottom get pushed out of the economy. A shortage of jobs or adequate wages, coupled with high housing costs, is the right blend of ingredients for homelessness.

FIGURE 3.7

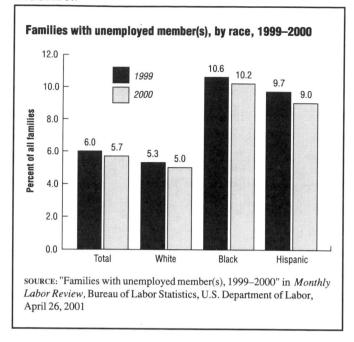

Families with unemployed member(s), by race, 1999–2000

SOURCE: "Families with unemployed member(s), 1999–2000" in *Monthly Labor Review,* Bureau of Labor Statistics, U.S. Department of Labor, April 26, 2001

TABLE 3.4

Comparison of personal characteristics of family head in working low-income, other low-income, and higher-income families, 1996

	Low-income families[a]		Higher-income families[c]
	Working[b]	Other	
Age (years)	35.5	37.7	40.6
Marital status (percent)			
Married	68.9	45.2	83.0
Widowed/divorced/separated	17.3	25.6	8.9
Never married	13.9	29.2	8.1
Male (percent)	63.0	43.0	73.4
Education (percent)			
Less than high school	22.4	35.2	4.3
HS grad or GED	45.7	39.3	35.0
Some college	21.5	17.9	24.7
College graduate	10.4	7.6	36.0
Has work-limiting condition (percent)	11.6	27.6	7.1
Race (percent)			
Black, non-Hispanic	18.0	26.5	9.4
Hispanic	11.6	10.7	3.9
White, non-Hispanic	66.0	56.2	82.5
Other	4.5	6.6	4.2

Note: Family head is the highest-earning adult, except in families with no earner for which the head is the adult with the most education.
[a] All families with incomes below 200 percent of the official poverty level.
[b] All families with incomes below 200 percent of the official poverty level in which the average annual hours worked per adult is at least 1,000.
[c] All families with income at 200 percent of the official poverty level or above.

SOURCE: Gregory Acs, Katherin Ross Phillips, and Daniel McKenzie, "Table 2: Comparison of Personal Characteristics of Family Head in Working Low-Income, Other Low-Income, and Higher-Income Families, 1996," in *On the Bottom Rung: A Profile of Americans in Low-Income Working Families,* Urban Institute, Washington, DC, October 2000

Unemployment

The official unemployment rates have been subject to considerable scrutiny and criticism over the years. Social and economic researchers believe that the rates misrepresent the actual numbers of people who cannot find work to support themselves and their families. For example, the official unemployment figures do not count those who have expired their unemployment benefits and are still not working. The figures also leave out those who are underemployed, such as the college graduate who takes a low-paying job or part-time job until he or she finds adequate employment. It is likely, then, that the true number of people who cannot find adequate employment is higher than official statistics indicate.

The U.S. Bureau of Labor Statistics reported that in May 2001 the official number of unemployed persons in the United States was 6.2 million, and the percentage of the labor-aged population of the United States that was jobless (the unemployment rate) was 4.4 percent. This 4.4 percent unemployment rate was down from 4.7 percent in May 2000, but is still .2 percent higher than it was in May 1999.

Unemployment is a permanent feature of the economy. It can never be entirely eliminated, since there will always be people who lose their jobs for various reasons, and it may take them some time to find new work even in the best of economic times. Historically speaking, an unemployment level of 4.4 percent is very low. This reflects the fact that the U.S. economy performed extremely well throughout most of the 1990s and into 2001. As of May 2001, the unemployment rate has been below 6.0 percent for over seven years.

Some segments of American society have experienced more unemployment than others. According to the U.S.

Bureau of Labor Statistics in 2000, of the nation's 71.7 million families, 5.7 percent reported having an unemployed member in an average week. The proportion of black families with an unemployed member (10.2 percent) was higher than the proportion for either Hispanic (9.0 percent) or white families (5.0 percent). Hispanic families had the largest drop in unemployment between 1999 and 2000, from 9.7 percent to 9.0 percent (Figure 3.7).

UNDEREMPLOYED OR DISCOURAGED WORKERS. In June of 2001 the Economic Policy Institute, an independent policy group, released a statement reporting that as the economy slowed over the previous few months, the size of the civilian labor force (the number of persons employed and unemployed) decreased. They said that this shrinkage might be the result of some people giving up on seeking work because of a perceived decline in employment opportunities. If economic growth had continued to rise over the months prior to June, the labor force would likely have grown by about 570,000. If these workers couldn't find jobs and ended up being counted as unemployed, rather than not being counted at all, the unemployment rate in May would have been 4.7 percent instead of the reported 4.4 percent (Economic Policy Institute, *Economic Snapshots,* June 2001).

The U.S. Census Bureau's Current Population Survey reported that about 1.1 million persons (not seasonally adjusted) were marginally attached to the labor force in May 2001, the same as a year earlier. These were people who wanted and were available for work and had looked for a job sometime in the prior 12 months. But since they had not searched for work in the four weeks preceding the survey, they were not counted as unemployed.

In an effort to bring more accuracy to the unemployment figures, the Census Bureau has begun to estimate the numbers of discouraged workers. Discouraged workers, a subgroup of the marginally attached, gave up looking for work specifically because they believed no jobs were available for them. In May 2001 the number of discouraged workers was counted as 325,000 (U.S. Census Bureau, *Current Population Survey,* May 2001).

The Working Poor

Many poor people work, including some homeless people. The Economic Policy Institute (EPI) has the following description of the definition of the working poor:

- Low-income workers who have a substantial commitment to the labor force.

- Low-income families struggling to meet all their expenses. (Working families are defined as those in which the adults work at least 1,000 hours a year, on average, roughly half-time work.)

The EPI reported that in the year 2000, 25 percent of all workers earned below poverty level wages (defined as the hourly wage a worker needs to lift a family of four out of poverty, equal to $8.19 an hour in 1999). Note that this is higher than the actual poverty level because some of these workers have other wage earners in the family, or have smaller families that require less money to support them.

The EPI also reports that the ratio of hourly wage for high-wage workers (95th percentile) to low-wage workers (10th percentile) in 1999 was: 5.5 to 1 (*The State of Working America 2000–01, Wage and Compensation Trends,* Economic Policy Institute, May 2001). The share of workers earning a poverty-level wage or lower grew over the 1980s and early 1990s, driven primarily by the decline in average wages for men. After 1995 the share of both male and female workers earning poverty wages fell, due to the improving economy.

The EPI study reveals that women are much more likely to earn low wages than men. In 2000, 31.1 percent of women earned poverty-level wages or less, significantly more than the share of men (19.5 percent). Women were also much less likely to earn very high wages in 1999—only 7.8 percent of women, but 15.8 percent of men, earned at least three times the poverty-level wage (*The State of Working America 2000–01, National Data,*

Wage and Compensation Trends, Economic Policy Institute, May 2000).

Results from an Urban Institute study of the working poor (Table 3.4) show that in terms of education, the heads of working families are in a slightly better position than their counterparts in other low-income families but much worse off than the heads of higher-income families. More than 22 percent of the heads of working poor families have less than a high school education compared with fewer than 5 percent of higher-income family heads. Only about 10 percent of working low-income family heads are college graduates, compared with 36 percent of higher-income family heads.

On the race/ethnicity dimension, fewer heads of working poor families than of other low-income families are black (18 versus 26.5 percent), but very similar percentages are Hispanic (11.6 versus 10.7 percent). Heads of working poor families are more likely to be white than the heads of other low-income families, but considerably less likely to be white than their higher-income counterparts (66.0 versus 82.5 percent).

Working poor families are more likely to have children and more likely to have more children than either persons in other low-income families or persons in higher-income families. For example, more than four-fifths of them (82.1 percent) live in families with children, compared with about two-thirds for the other two groups. About 80 percent of the working poor living in families with children have more than one child, compared with about 75 percent for persons in other low-income families and about 65 percent for those in higher-income families. (*On the Bottom Rung, A Profile of Americans in Low-Income Working Families,* Urban Institute, October 2000.)

THE DECREASE IN THE REAL VALUE OF EARNINGS. As the U.S. economy's growth faltered in early 2001, the inflation-adjusted weekly earnings of most workers have grown more slowly, even slipping into slightly negative territory in the first quarter of 2001. At the same time, a significant gap between productivity and wages has resurfaced, suggesting a potential return to growth in wage inequality. (See Figure 3.8.) Note that in early 2001, real wages are growing in a direction opposite from productivity.

The data shows yearly changes in both productivity and the real weekly earnings of nonsupervisory, production workers. These workers—blue-collar manufacturing and service workers—comprise 80 percent of the private sector workforce. As the recession of the 1980s receded and the economy improved in the early 1990s, real weekly earnings stopped declining, eventually rising along with productivity around 1997–98. Typically when the real wages and productivity grow at a similar rate, it means that workers are sharing in the profits from their labor; they can also purchase the products they make or

FIGURE 3.8

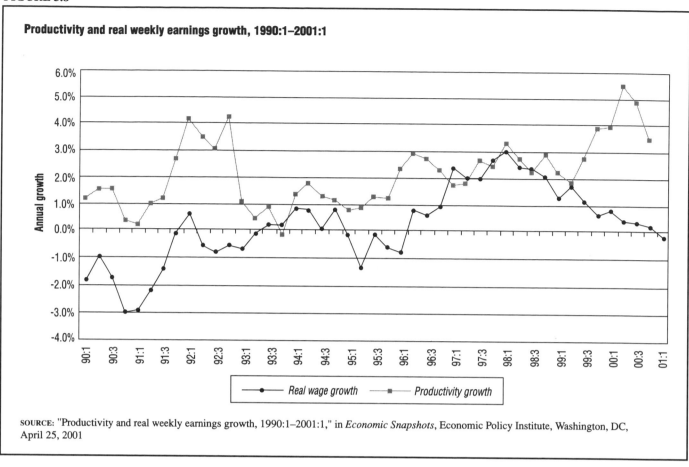

Productivity and real weekly earnings growth, 1990:1–2001:1

SOURCE: "Productivity and real weekly earnings growth, 1990:1–2001:1," in *Economic Snapshots*, Economic Policy Institute, Washington, DC, April 25, 2001

serve. By 1999, however, real weekly earnings growth began to fall, due mostly to faster price growth and fewer hours of work per week. In the quarter, 2001 Q:1, real earnings declined slightly. Meanwhile, productivity continued to grow at historically high rates. These differences led to the gap between the earnings and output evident in Figure 3.8. If this trend continues, working-class families will face both lower earnings and higher inequality.

WELFARE REFORM AND THE POOR

In 1996 the passage of the Personal Responsibility and Work Opportunity Reconciliation Act (PL 104-193), the most sweeping welfare legislation since the 1960s, ended Aid to Families with Dependent Children (AFDC) and gave the states control over the administration of benefits in the form of Temporary Aid to Needy Families (TANF) grants. In addition, the law made significant changes to Supplemental Security Income (SSI) and Medicaid.

Furthermore, several states reduced or eliminated General Assistance (GA) benefits for single poor people. That this reduction adds to the increase in homelessness was well proven in the results of a study by researchers Mark Greenberg and Jim Baumohl. In their research, published in 1996, Greenberg and Braumohl show that increases in outlays of GA benefits directly reduced homelessness. (Green-

berg and Baumohl, *Income Maintenance: Little Help Now, Less on the Way, Homelessness in America,* National Coalition for the Homeless, Oryx Press, 1996)

Returning Local Control

The Temporary Assistance for Needy Families (TANF) block grant legislation (the welfare reform initiative) was designed to fulfill two primary objectives:

• Return more control of relief assistance programs to the state governments—This grants the states great flexibility to design whatever mix of services and benefits they think will reduce dependency and provide for the needy.

• Limit the amount of time a person spent on public assistance—Specifically, the 1996 law contains a five-year lifetime limit on receipt of federally funded cash assistance; authorizes states to impose shorter time limits at their discretion; requires that, by the year 2002, 50 percent of all recipients who have received cash aid for two years work at least 30 hours a week in order to continue receiving benefits.

Many people agree that these are worthy goals. Local authorities are clearly better equipped to determine the needs of the people in their area than a distant federal government. Each state has specific needs; geography, climate,

FIGURE 3.9

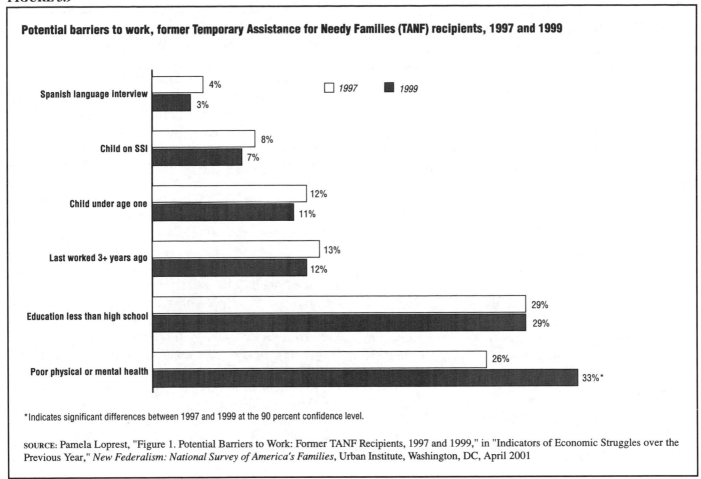

Potential barriers to work, former Temporary Assistance for Needy Families (TANF) recipients, 1997 and 1999

*Indicates significant differences between 1997 and 1999 at the 90 percent confidence level.

SOURCE: Pamela Loprest, "Figure 1. Potential Barriers to Work: Former TANF Recipients, 1997 and 1999," in "Indicators of Economic Struggles over the Previous Year," *New Federalism: National Survey of America's Families*, Urban Institute, Washington, DC, April 2001

and ethnicity all vary from state to state, and all deserve individual consideration. The second focus, to encourage work instead of public assistance, is also respectful of the needs of the individual and society to advance themselves. Many critics of the old system felt that it unintentionally discouraged welfare recipients from working. Working brings in money, but it also creates new expenses, such as commuting to and from work and child care. Since most welfare recipients were qualified only for low-paying jobs, they often found that these expenses left them with less money than they would have had if they simply stayed on welfare, even though that meant they had no prospect of ever leaving poverty. The welfare-to-work initiative has another, residual benefit as well: not only does it aim to benefit the recipient, the chances that the children of the recipient will be impoverished as an adult are lowered.

But there is one wrinkle worth giving a shake: both these objectives reflect the attitudes of the English Poor Laws of feudal times. The first, local responsibility for the poor, has historically proven to result in discriminatory practices—from medieval England through colonial times. It lends itself to subjective and/or punitive practices. The second objective resembles the deserving/undeserving moral judgments of the poor. It was in applying these same qualifications that the poorhouses were born.

There are reasons to be concerned about welfare reform, however. While local control makes it easier to address the specific needs of the poor in particular areas, it also makes it possible for localities to restrict benefits in ways that a nationwide program would never be able to. The welfare reform laws do place some limits on local authorities, but it remains necessary for people concerned with equal justice to remain alert to possible violations. There is also an inherent assumption that anyone who really wants work will be able to find some, and that anyone who cannot find work within a specified period must not really be trying and doesn't deserve any government aid. This ignores the fact that many people on welfare, and poor people in general, lack the skills or education necessary for most jobs. The homeless, who do not even have a fixed address, telephone, or clean clothes for an interview, are especially vulnerable in this system.

LIFE AFTER WELFARE REFORM. By 2001 welfare reform had been more successful than its many critics expected. Welfare rolls had declined by roughly half since the early 1990s, and employment rates had risen for most former (and many current) welfare recipients. How much of these positive results were due to the economic boom of the 1990s, with the accompanying increase in jobs, remains yet to be determined. The most significant data will emerge when the economy turns downward, and a recession begins.

Researchers know that there have been declines in the welfare rolls. But as of yet, they don't know what happened to the people who are missing from the files. Major studies are now underway. To get a look at what information is available, and what the welfare reform act meant to people whose lives were directly affected, Sheila Zedlewski and Donald Alderson of the Urban Institute, analyzed current data and presented the following preliminary results of the AFDC to TANF reform measures in April 2001:

• The proportion of single mothers on welfare who reported living with partners increased

• The proportion of African Americans on welfare who reported living with partners increased

• The proportion of adults on welfare who worked for pay rose

• The proportion of recipients who were new entrants to the welfare system was about the same, despite some new state programs that attempt to divert adults from enrolling in TANF

• Adults on TANF in 1999 were no more disadvantaged than those on TANF in 1997

• Longer-term welfare recipients were significantly more disadvantaged than the new entrants

• The proportion of recipients blocked from access to the workforce due to less than high school education was the same (29 percent) in 1997 and 1999 (Figure 3.9).

This analysis is based on a comparison of 1,831 families on TANF in 1997 and 850 families in 1999, representing 2.2 million and 1.5 million families, respectively. The characteristics and work activities presented were obtained from interviewing the adult most knowledgeable about the children in the family, usually the mother. (Sheila Zedlewski and Donald Alderson, *Families on Welfare in the Post-TANF Era: Do They Differ from Their Pre-TANF Counterparts?* Paper presented at the American Economics Association meeting, New Orleans, January 2001.)

EMPLOYMENT AND THE HOMELESS

It is extremely difficult for the homeless to escape their condition without a job. Yet it is equally difficult for the homeless to find and keep good jobs. Many barriers stand in their way, including: a lack of transportation or child care, a stable address or telephone number, cleanliness and proper appearance. Many homeless people also have a poor education, and few have marketable skills. These difficulties can sometimes be addressed and helped by homeless employment programs, shelters, and state employment agencies. A less easily remedied, but poten-

tially more powerful barrier to exiting homelessness is the state of the labor market. The availability of jobs and the wages paid for the available jobs often determine whether or not people can remove themselves from homelessness.

Wage Barriers to Exiting Homelessness

During the 1970s U.S. manufacturing industries began closing down and heading for cheaper labor markets abroad. For the last hundred years, America had been primarily an industrial nation, and the loss of industry created a gap in the economy. This gap was filled by the services and information industries. These industries, especially the service industry, do not pay particularly well. The Bureau of Labor Statistics shows that of occupations at or below minimum wage (Table 3.5), by group, the technical services field, with 23 million jobs, has the highest number of workers. This field includes such jobs as: telemarketers, receptionists, answering service personnel, and data entry workers—information service jobs. Following low-paying manufacturing-related jobs with almost 15 million, is the third largest group, the service occupations with 13.5 million workers. Combined with the tech services jobs, the total number of service industry jobs is 36.5 million. As Table 3.5 shows, these jobs provide barely enough income to be considered subsistence wages, yet represent the largest group of available employment opportunities. (Bureau of Labor Statistics, *Employment and Earnings,* January 2001)

In the service industry occupations, nearly 11 percent of all workers who worked in a service job for at least six months out of the year were poor. This indicates that longevity in a service job does not guarantee higher wages. Service industry jobs tend to level out the amount of wages paid, holding even longer-term employees in poverty. Other occupations with relatively high proportions of workers in poverty included farming, forestry, and fishing (15.7 percent), and operators, fabricators, and laborers (6.9 percent). (*A Profile of the Working Poor 1999,* U.S. Department of Labor, Bureau of Labor Statistics, February 2001)

In February 2001 the Bureau of Labor Statistics released a report examining the occupation constructs of the poor person's life. The report states that the risk of being among the working poor increases significantly for workers who have not completed high school. As the education levels become higher, the percentages in poverty become smaller. This is bad news for the typical homeless person, as most of the homeless are very poorly educated. Only 28 percent have an education beyond high school, and 38 percent have not even completed high school.

Of the homeless respondents from the Urban Institute's 1996 study, 44 percent reported working in the previous month (Table 3.6). Two percent earned income as

TABLE 3.5

Wage and salary workers paid hourly rates with earnings at or below the prevailing federal minimum wage by occupation and industry (Numbers in thousands)

Occupation and industry	2000				
	Workers paid hourly rates				
		Below prevailing federal minimum wage	At prevailing federal minimum wage	Total at or below prevailing federal minimum wage	
	Total			Number	Percent of hourly-paid workers
Occupation					
Managerial and professional specialty	10,049	79	33	112	1.1
Executive, administrative, and managerial	4,280	35	12	47	1.1
Professional specialty	5,769	44	20	65	1.1
Technical, sales, and administrative support	23,020	229	262	491	2.1
Technicians and related support	2,790	12	6	17	.6
Sales occupations	7,472	131	156	286	3.8
Administrative support, including clerical	12,758	86	101	187	1.5
Service occupations	13,524	1,302	374	1,676	12.4
Private household	361	61	5	65	18.1
Protective service	1,550	17	7	24	1.6
Service, except private household and protective	11,613	1,224	362	1,587	13.7
Food service workers	5,564	1,046	218	1,264	22.7
Health service workers	2,159	37	38	75	3.5
Cleaning and building service workers	2,450	63	49	112	4.6
Personal service workers	1,440	79	57	136	9.4
Precision production, craft, and repair	9,811	37	18	55	.6
Operators, fabricators, and laborers	14,933	162	146	308	2.1
Machine operators, assemblers, and inspectors	6,374	45	45	90	1.4
Transportation and material moving occupations	3,662	42	17	60	1.6
Handlers, equipment cleaners, helpers, and laborers	4,897	75	84	150	3.2
Farming, forestry, and fishing	1,407	34	34	68	4.8
Industry					
Private wage and salary workers	63,951	1,754	789	2,543	4.0
Agriculture	1,241	29	26	55	4.4
Nonagricultural industries	62,710	1,725	763	2,488	4.0
Mining	297	1	1	1	.4
Construction	4,915	15	14	29	.6
Manufacturing	12,851	64	58	122	.9
Durable goods	7,869	36	18	54	.7
Nondurable goods	4,982	28	40	68	1.4
Transportation and public utilities	4,284	43	16	59	1.4
Transportation	2,729	35	10	45	1.6
Communications and other public utilities	1,555	8	6	14	.9
Wholesale and retail trade	17,946	1,184	420	1,604	8.9
Wholesale trade	2,416	19	9	28	1.2
Retail trade	15,530	1,164	412	1,576	10.1
Eating and drinking places	5,325	1,007	234	1,241	23.3
Finance, insurance, and real estate	2,877	20	14	33	1.2
Services	19,540	399	240	640	3.3
Private households	430	65	6	71	16.6
Other service industries	19,110	334	234	568	3.0
Personal services, except private households	1,849	85	31	116	6.3
Entertainment and recreation services	1,256	62	32	94	7.5
Government workers	8,793	89	78	167	1.9
Federal	1,828	10	9	19	1.1
State	2,284	24	27	52	2.3
Local	4,680	55	41	96	2.1

Note: The prevailing federal minimum wage was $5.15 per hour in 2000. Data are for wage and salary workers, excluding the incorporated self-employed. They refer to a person's earnings on their sole or principal job, and pertain only to workers who are paid hourly rates. Salaried workers and other nonhourly workers are not included. The presence of workers with hourly earnings below the minimum wage does not necessarily indicate violations of the Fair Labor Standards Act, as there are exceptions to the minimum wage provisions of the law. In addition, some survey respondents might have rounded the hourly earnings to the nearest dollar, and, as a result, reported hourly earnings below the minimum wage even though they earned the minimum wage or higher.

SOURCE: "Wage and salary workers paid hourly rates with earnings at or below the prevailing Federal minimum wage by occupation and industry," Bureau of Labor Statistics, Employment and Earnings, January 2001

self-employed entrepreneurs—by peddling or selling belongings—leaving 42 percent of the homeless respondents who worked for and were paid by an employer. Since 96 percent of the employed homeless people in the Urban Institute study earned their wages in a manner that gave others control over their income, it underscores the strong dependency working homeless people have on the wages and conditions of the labor market.

TABLE 3.6

Income levels, income sources, and employment, by homeless status

	Currently Homeless Clients (N = 2938)	Formerly Homeless Clients (N = 677)	Other Service Users (N = 518)
Mean Income from All Sources (Last 30 Days)[1]	$367	$470	$575
Median Income from All Sources (Last 30 Days)[1]	300	462	514
Income from All Sources over Last 30 Days			
None	13(%)	5(%)	5(%)
Less than $100	17	9	6
$100 to $299	19	16	10
$300 to $499	18	30	25
$500 to $699	14	20	21
$700 to $799	4	6	7
$800 to $999	5	6	7
$1,000 to $1,199	3	2	3
$1,200 or more	4	5	12
No answer	3	1	2
Did Any Paid Work at All in Last 30 Days	44	34	28
Sources of Earned Income in Last 30 Days			
Job lasting 3 or more months	13	14	16
Job expected to last 3 or more months	7	7	4
Temporary job, nonfarm work	8	6	3
Temporary job, farm work	3	*	1
Day job or pick-up job	14	5	5
Peddling or selling personal belongings	2	2	*
Received Money/Benefits from Government Sources in Last 30 Days			
Aid to Families with Dependent Children (AFDC)	10	8	10
Aid to Families with Dependent Children (AFDC) only families with children	52	45	45
General Assistance	9	16	7
Supplemental Security Income	11	29	26
Social Security Disability Insurance (SSDI)	8	16	10
Social Security	3	6	33
Veteran's disability payments (veterans only)	6	14	23
Veteran's pension (not disability related—veterans only)	2	1	16
Food stamps	37	48	37
Received Means-Tested Government Benefits[2]			
Any including food stamps	45	70	56
Any other than food stamps	28	57	47
Other Sources of Income over the Last 30 Days			
Parents	9	4	6
Friends (includes boyfriends or girlfriends)	12	9	5
Asking for money on the streets	8	3	*

*Denotes values that are less than 0.5 but greater than 0 percent.
[1]If an income range was reported by client, mid-point of range was used in calculating mean.
[2]AFDC, GA, SSI, food stamps, housing assistance.

SOURCE: "Table 3.8: Income Levels, Income Sources, and Employment, by Homeless Status," in *Homelessness: Programs and the People They Serve: Findings of the National Survey of Homeless Assistance Providers and Clients*, Urban Institute, Washington, DC, December 1999

Advocates for the homeless are concerned that this dependency, combined with the current labor market conditions, actually supports continued homelessness. Since the majority of homeless people do not have more than a high-school education, and since a majority of the low-paying jobs go to those without more than a high-school education, advocates worry that the available job opportunities for homeless people are insufficient for exiting homelessness. The argument is that to have to rely upon poverty-level wages to provide enough income to meet the daily costs of living and also to meet the financial needs of acquiring housing (i.e. security deposit, prepaid rent, utility start-up fees, etc.) is extremely difficult.

WORK FOR THE HOMELESS

It costs money to live. Even homeless people have needs that can only be met with money. From needing something as simple as a toothbrush or a meal, to money for a newspaper and to call job prospects, homeless people need money to begin to improve their lives. Out of the need to survive, homeless people have come up with a number of ways to earn money, weaving their ventures among local ordinances, public opinion, and the labor market.

Street Newspapers: Bootstrap Initiatives

All across the United States as well as overseas, homeless people are publishing, writing for, and selling their own newspapers. The State Historical Society of Wisconsin reported 46 homeless newspapers in the United States in 1995.

Many street newspaper publishers belong to a professional organization, the North American Street Newspaper Association (NASNA), organized in Chicago in 1996. NASNA holds an annual conference, offers business advice and services, and supports street newspaper publishers in the same way that any professional organization supports its membership. They also lobby the government on homeless issues.

Generally, the street newspapers are loaned on credit to homeless vendors who then sell them for one to two dollars apiece. At the end of the workday, the vendor pays the publisher the agreed-upon price and pockets the remainder as profit. For example, Boston's *Spare Change* newspaper publishes 12,000 copies every two weeks. Vendors purchase newspapers for 25 cents apiece and resell them for $1.00, pocketing $.75 for each paper sold. New York City's *Street News* gives the vendors ten free copies and allows them to earn $1.40 from each paper sold at $2.00.

This cooperative arrangement between publishers, vendors, and consumers has many benefits:

• Creation of jobs

• Supports the work ethic

• Accommodates the mobility of homeless people

• Provides reliable employment despite crisis living conditions

• Informs the public about homelessness

• Erases stereotypes of the drunken, illiterate, "unworthy" homeless person

• Gives the writers and vendors a sense of accomplishment

• Provides immediate cash to those who need it most.

Most of the homeless newspaper vendors are not been able to earn enough just from selling newspapers to move themselves form homelessness, but as the quality and availability of these publications grow, homeless people envision the street newspaper industry as becoming a means to moving tens of thousands from homelessness.

THE STREET NEWS, NEW YORK CITY. The earliest known homeless publication, *The Street News,* was launched in 1989 by the New York Times and the New York Metropolitan Transportation Authority. By 1991, when the publication suffered from a scandal involving misuse of funds, *The Street News* was boasting some 25,000 copies per issue, which then fell to 8,000. By 2000 circulation was back up to 20,000. The paper is known for its radical political stance and unusual stories.

SPARE CHANGE, BOSTON. Begun in 1992 as one of the nation's first street newspapers to benefit the homeless, *Spare Change* is published every other week by the Homeless Empowerment Project (HEP) in Cambridge, Massachusetts. Its stated mission is to "play a role in ending homelessness in our community by providing income, skill development and self-advocacy opportunities to people who are homeless or at risk of homelessness." The newspaper provides a forum for creative expression and advocacy for homeless individuals. Along with the production, distribution, and sale of the street newspaper, HEP operates a training center for teaching computer skills to the homeless. They also sponsor a writer's workshop and promote a speaker's bureau.

Day Labor

Regular work, characterized by a permanent and ongoing relationship between employer and employee, does not figure significantly in the lives and routines of most homeless, as it is usually unavailable or inaccessible. Homelessness makes getting and keeping regular work difficult due to the lack of a fixed address, communication, and, in many cases, the inability to get a good night's sleep, clean up, and dress appropriately. Studies have found that the longer a person is homeless, the less likely he or she is to pursue wage labor and the more likely that person is to engage in some other form of work. For those who do participate in regular jobs, in most cases the wages received are not sufficient to escape from living on the street.

Day labor, wage labor secured on a day-to-day basis, typically at lower wages and changing locations, is somewhat easier for the homeless to secure. Day labor may involve unloading trucks, cleaning up warehouses, cutting grass, or washing windows. Day labor often fits the abilities of the homeless because transportation may be provided to the work site, and appearance, work history, and references are less important. Equally attractive to a homeless person, day labor usually pays cash at quitting time, thus providing immediate pocket money. Day labor jobs are, however, by definition, without a future. They can provide survival on the street, but are not generally sufficient to get a person off the street. Consequently, many homeless turn to shadow work.

Shadow Work

Shadow work refers to methods of getting money that are outside the normal economy, some of them illegal. These methods include panhandling, scavenging, selling possessions, picking up cans and selling them, selling one's blood or plasma, theft, or peddling illegal goods, drugs, or services. A homeless person seldom engages in all of these activities consistently but may turn to some of them, as needed. Researchers estimate that 60 percent of the homeless engage in some shadow work. Shadow work is more common for homeless men than homeless women. Theft is more common for younger homeless persons.

FIGURE 3.10

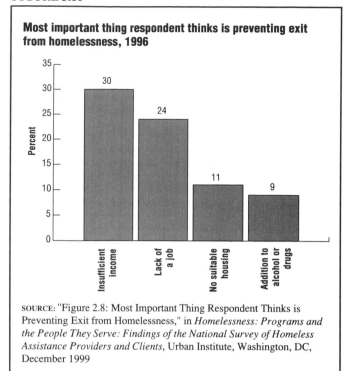

Most important thing respondent thinks is preventing exit from homelessness, 1996

SOURCE: "Figure 2.8: Most Important Thing Respondent Thinks is Preventing Exit from Homelessness," in *Homelessness: Programs and the People They Serve: Findings of the National Survey of Homeless Assistance Providers and Clients*, Urban Institute, Washington, DC, December 1999

FIGURE 3.11

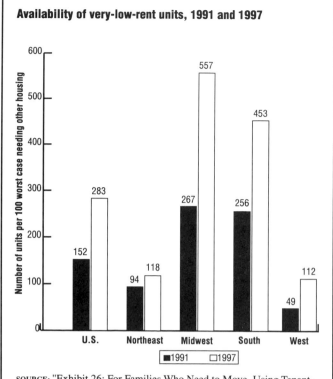

Availability of very-low-rent units, 1991 and 1997

SOURCE: "Exhibit 26: For Families Who Need to Move, Using Tenant-Based Assistance Became Easier in Each Region Between 1991 and 1997," in *Rental Housing Assistance—The Worsening Crisis: A Report to Congress on Worst Case Housing Needs*, U.S. Department of Housing and Urban Development, Washington, DC, March 2000

Survival on the streets is usually managed by a mixture of institutionalized assistance, wage labor, and shadow work. Studies have found that many homeless people are very resourceful in surviving the rigors of street life and recommend that this resourcefulness be somehow channeled into training that can lead to jobs paying a living wage. Some observers suggest, however, that homeless people who have adapted to street life may likely need transitional socialization programs as much as programs that teach them a marketable skill.

Institutionalized Assistance

Institutionalized assistance refers to "established or routine monetary assistance patterned in accordance with tradition, legislation, or organizations" (David Snow, Leon Anderson, Theron Quist, and Daniel Cress, *Material Survival Strategies on the Street: Homeless People as Bricoleurs, Homelessness in America,* edited by the National Coalition for the Homeless, Oryx Press, 1996). This would include institutionalized labor, such as provided by soup kitchens, shelters, and rehabilitation programs that sometimes pay the homeless for work related to facility operation. The number of people employed by these agencies is a small percentage of the homeless population. In addition, the pay—room, board, and a small stipend—tends to tie the homeless to the organization rather than providing the means to get off the street.

Institutionalized assistance also includes income supplements provided by government, family, and friends. According to the *Homelessness in America* study, while a considerable number of the homeless may receive some financial help from family or friends, it is usually small. Women seem to receive more help from family and friends and to remain on the streets for shorter periods of time than men. Cash from family and friends seems to decline with the amount of time spent on the street and with age.

EXITING HOMELESSNESS

The further down someone has fallen in his or her life circumstances, the harder it is to get up. This is particularly true of the homeless. The 1996 Urban Institute study revealed that homeless people say that the primary reason they cannot exit homelessness is insufficient income (Figure 3.10). Of those clients surveyed, 54 percent cited employment-related reasons for why they remained homeless (insufficient income, 30 percent; lack of a job, 24 percent).

Table 3.6 illustrates the lack of income experienced by the currently homeless. Eighty-one percent of the currently homeless had incomes of less than $700 in the 30 days before the study. It is to be noted that the 4 percent with incomes of $1,200 or more, while seemingly a lot of income by comparison, would have a difficult time affording housing and living expenses in today's economy. This may explain why they are still homeless, despite having such a significantly higher income than the majority (63 percent) of homeless people who had incomes of less than half that amount. Most in the study were receiving their income from Aid to Families with Dependent Children (now referred to as TANF). Of formerly homeless people surveyed, the median income of $470 would amount to an annual income of $5,640, an amount well below even the lowest poverty level limit. This extreme poverty indicates the likelihood of reoccurring homelessness.

These income levels clearly demonstrate the financial difficulty a homeless person encounters in trying to permanently exit homelessness or poverty on personal income alone. Just as the government spending on elderly programs has made the lives of those over 65 significantly better, government spending applied to programs for the poor would raise them out of poverty, making their lives easier as well. The graph from a Housing and Urban Development (HUD) study, Figure 3.11, shows that families with the benefit of government sponsored tenant assistance had an easier time moving in all regions of the nation as compared to 1991 when less funding was available. (*Rental Housing Assistance—The Worsening Crisis, A Report to Congress on Worst Case Housing Needs,* Housing and Urban Development, 2000)

CHAPTER 4
THE HOUSING PROBLEM

Once, the word "home" meant the place where some-one lived with a family. People without family ties were considered homeless no matter where they lived. Under such a definition, American sociologists once described men who lived in skid-row hotels as homeless; they lived alone and seldom saw their kin. After 1960, however, more and more Americans began living alone by choice. Hence, a home became a fixed address where one could leave his or her possessions, come and go at will, and sleep undisturbed. Since 1980 most Americans have adopted an even less demanding view of home. Today, any private space intended for sleeping can qualify as a home, as long as those who sleep there have a legal right to be there and can exclude strangers. As a result, the homeless became those people who had no fixed address and no private space of their own, however temporary.

The obvious solution to homelessness would be to find a home for everyone who needs one. There is plenty of housing available in the United States, certainly enough to shelter every single soul, if it was free. The problem lies in the affordability of that housing. Most of the housing in the United States costs far more than someone in poverty can afford to rent or buy. For the poorest members of society, it can be difficult, or sometimes outright impossible, to pay the rent on even the cheapest housing available, driving these people into homelessness.

THE PRIMARY REASON FOR HOMELESSNESS

Research indicates that the primary cause of most homelessness is a simple inability to pay for housing, caused by some combination of low income and high housing costs. While many other factors may contribute to homelessness, such as a poor education or mental illness, addressing these problems will seldom bring someone out of homelessness by itself. The underlying issue of not being able to afford housing will still need to be addressed.

New York University (NYU) researchers conducted a study indicating that no real difference exists between homeless people and the rest of society, other than housing affordability issues. Funded by the National Institute of Mental Health, the NYU team conducted a five-year study of 564 homeless families. In *Predictors of Homelessness Among Families in New York City: From Shelter Request to Housing Stability* (November 1998), they presented their results.

The research team found that when homeless families were provided with subsidies that allowed them to afford housing, 80 percent of these formerly homeless families remained housed in their own residence for at least a year. This was true regardless of their social or personal attributes, such as their education level, race, or sex. This confirms the idea that, while many homeless people face difficulties due to their personal backgrounds, these problems are not what drove most of them into homelessness. Furthermore, if they can be put in a position where housing is affordable to them, most will be able to take advantage of it.

THE LACK OF LOW-INCOME HOUSING

Broadly speaking, low-income housing is housing that is affordable to those in poverty. The federal government's official standard for low-income housing is that it should cost no more than 30 percent of the annual income of someone in poverty. This includes the cost of utilities. In 2001 a family of two people with an annual income of less than $11,234 was in poverty, a family of four was in poverty if their income was less than $17,601 (Table 3.1, Chapter 3). Thus in 2001, low-income housing for a family of two should cost no more than $281 a month; for a family of four it should cost no more than $440 a month.

Researchers from every discipline agree that the number of housing units that are affordable to the poor is insufficient to meet needs. The National League of Cities,

TABLE 4.1

Opinions of city officials polled by the National League of Cities

In which of the priority areas listed below do you think the federal government and the new presidential administration should devote the most new attention and significant resources toward helping American communities achieve their true potential? (List your top 3.)

Investing in regional economic and workforce development	67%
Increasing the availability of affordable housing	28%
Revitalizing and redeveloping neighborhoods	28%
Supporting local and regional "smart growth" or growth management strategies	34%
Investing in infrastructure (roads/transit, water, sewer)	67%
Investing in public education and other supports for children, youth, and families	65%
Protecting natural resources and local environmental quality	2%

SOURCE: "12. In which of the priority areas listed below do you think the federal government and the new Presidential Administration should devote the most new attention and significant resources toward helping American communities achieve their true potential?" in *State of America's Cities: The Seventeenth Annual Opinion Survey of Municipal Elected Officials*, National League of Cities, Washington, DC, January 2001

in its fifteenth annual opinion survey of municipal elected officials (*The State of America's Cities*, 2000), found that 28 percent of city officials believed that President George W. Bush should devote the most attention to increasing the availability of affordable housing (Table 4.1). In response to a similar question two years ago, only 3 percent of those officials said they would want to address Congress about housing in their cities. In 2000 the U.S. Conference of Mayors surveyed 25 major cities and found that in those cities, low-income households spent an average of 51 percent of their income on housing. The Joint Center for Housing Studies of Harvard University, in its publication, *The State of the Nation's Housing: 2001*, stated that over 14 million owner and renter households spent more than half their income on housing in 1999. They also found that there were 3.9 million poor renters or home owners—with an income equivalent to that of a full-time worker earning the minimum wage—who spent more than half their income on housing.

A Study of Those Most at Risk of Becoming Homeless

In March 2000 the Office of Policy Development and Research and the U.S. Department of Housing and Urban Development (HUD) released the results of an in-depth study of worst-care housing needs (*Rental Housing Assistance—The Worsening Crisis*, Office of Policy Development and Research, U.S. Department of Housing and Urban Development, March 2000). In the study, families who have "worst-case needs" are defined as those who:

- Are renters

- Do not receive housing assistance from federal, state, or local government programs

- Have incomes below 50 percent of their local area median family income, as determined by HUD

- Pay more than one-half of their income for rent and utilities, or live in severely substandard housing.

In other words these are extremely impoverished people who do not own their housing and can barely afford to pay their housing costs, or can only afford to stay in the very worst housing. Of all the people who have housing, they are the ones closest to being forced into homelessness. The study found that 5.4 million Americans had worst-case housing needs in 1997. This was an all-time high, with 600,000 more worst-case-needs households than in 1991. Among the report's key findings are:

- Despite economic expansion, worst-case-housing needs increased by 4 percent in the two years between 1995 and 1997.

- Families with worst-case needs are working harder than ever. Between 1991 and 1997, worst-case needs increased more than three times as fast among very low-income families with full-time wage earners than among very low-income families without full-time wage earners.

- The concentration of worst-case housing needs among poorest families rose from 1991 through 1997. By 1997 over three-fourths of those with worst-case needs had incomes more than 30 percent below the median in their area.

- Worst-case housing needs increased dramatically in minority households during the 1990s. Increases were particularly high among Hispanics and working minority families with children.

- Reflecting housing market pressures from population and job growth, declines in units affordable to extremely low-income families were greatest in the suburbs during the 1990s. Accordingly, poor families living in the suburbs most frequently faced worst-case needs. Over one-third of worst case households live in the suburbs.

For as long as worst-case needs have been reported, affordability rather than housing quality has been the main problem facing renters. In 1997, 94 percent of households with worst-case problems paid more than 50 percent of their income for rent. As Figure 4.1 illustrates, severe rent burden was the only housing problem for 77.3 percent of the families with worst-case needs. Another 13.8 percent not only paid more than half their income for rent, but lived in housing with moderate problems, and an additional 3.1 percent paid more than half their income to live in severely substandard housing. Only 5.9 percent of worst-case housing needs were due solely to problems with the housing unrelated to cost. What all of this means is that if assistance was made available to those with worst-case housing needs, or their rents lowered, then more than three-quarters of them would no longer have a worst-case housing need at all.

Reasons for the Lack of Low-Income Housing

The basic problem is that low-income housing does not make very much money for its landlords. Landlords naturally want to charge the highest rents that they can to maximize their profits. If their housing is nice enough so that they can charge a high rent, they will not hesitate to do so. If their housing is not so nice, and the best rent they can charge for it is low, then in many cases they will either try to improve its value so they can raise the rent, or simply stop renting the housing at all. Martha Burt, in the 1992 study, *Over the Edge: The Growth of Homelessness in the 1980s,* cited three factors that reduce the supply of low-cost rental housing:

- Disinvestment—the refusal or inability to repair and keep up the rental property, so that over time it falls into decay and becomes uninhabitable. In extreme cases, property owners have been known to burn down buildings rather than continue their upkeep.

- Abandonment—a situation in which the owner of the property defaults on ownership, refusing to pay mortgage payments, taxes, or other civic fees. Because of these defaults, the property reverts to the mortgage holder or the government, which may or may not be able or willing to continue operating the property as low-cost housing. In some cases, the property may sit empty for a long time before being sold or reopened for housing.

- Conversion—when low-income housing units, government-subsidized units or otherwise, are converted to other purposes such as condominiums, offices, retail stores, or warehouses. Research indicates that many lost units have been made unavailable to low-income renters because owners have "opted-out" of their government contracts to cash in on the lucrative, high-cost rental market, a process often called gentrification. It caters to the needs of the upper classes or gentry. (*Over the Edge: The Growth of Homelessness in the 1980s,* The Russell Sage Foundation, 1992).

The same problem of poor profits means that there is little incentive to build new units oriented at people with a low income. So when new units are built, they are almost always for people with moderate to high incomes. Then, after the units have become older and worn down, and they can only be rented for relatively small profits, they are often eliminated or renovated, to be replaced with more new housing for higher income people. Even housing built with or subsidized by federal funds tends to undergo this process—the higher profits are enough to compensate landlords for the penalties that they face for doing so.

AN EXAMPLE: ST. PAUL, MINNESOTA. A housing research project conducted in 2000 by the Wilder Research Center of St. Paul, Minnesota, illustrated how many trends converged to limit the supply of low-income housing in the region:

FIGURE 4.1

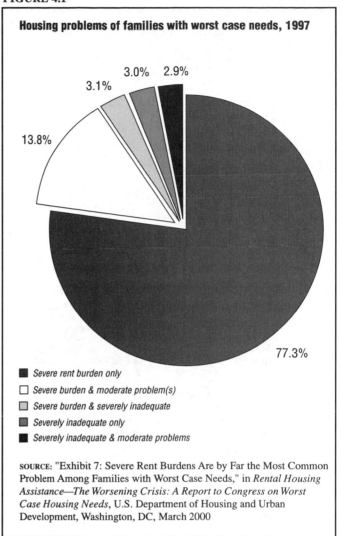

Housing problems of families with worst case needs, 1997

13.8%
3.1%
3.0%
2.9%
77.3%

- ■ *Severe rent burden only*
- □ *Severe burden & moderate problem(s)*
- ▨ *Severe burden & severely inadequate*
- ▤ *Severely inadequate only*
- ■ *Severely inadequate & moderate problems*

SOURCE: "Exhibit 7: Severe Rent Burdens Are by Far the Most Common Problem Among Families with Worst Case Needs," in *Rental Housing Assistance—The Worsening Crisis: A Report to Congress on Worst Case Housing Needs*, U.S. Department of Housing and Urban Development, Washington, DC, March 2000

- The regional economic boom—The strong economy draws people to the area for work, creating a higher demand for housing and driving up prices.

- All-time-high home ownership—Low mortgage rates lead to increased home ownership and an increased demand for new homes, at the expense of further construction of apartments and rental units.

- Decline in federal housing subsidies—With government cutbacks, housing developers who once relied on outside funding now prefer to compete in the hot housing market.

- Suburban growth—New housing is in the suburbs and focuses on upscale, not affordable, housing.

- Property taxes—leading to higher rents. Renters pay more taxes per square foot than homeowners, absorbing the higher tax burden passed on through rent costs.

- Aging housing stock—A large portion of affordable housing money goes towards maintenance, repair, and renovation, which is less for new units.

FIGURE 4.2

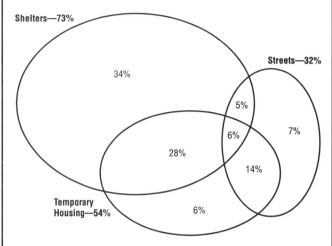

Where homeless clients slept on day of interview and previous seven days*

*Client used option at least once during the eight days including the day of the interview and the seven previous days, including being sampled at the site. "Shelters" = emergency and transitional shelters and voucher programs; "Streets" = any place not meant for habitation; "Temporary Housing" = own or other person's house, apartment, or room, including hotel/motel room that client paid for, but without the possibility of sleeping there for the next month without being asked to leave.

SOURCE: "Figure 2.13: Where Homeless Clients Slept on Day of Interview and Previous Seven Days," in *Homelessness: Programs and the People They Serve: Findings of the National Survey of Homeless Assistance Providers and Clients,* Urban Institute, Washington, DC, December 1999

FIGURE 4.3

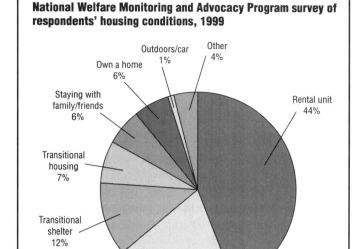

National Welfare Monitoring and Advocacy Program survey of respondents' housing conditions, 1999

SOURCE: "Figure 6: Respondents Housing Conditions: Almost 50% living homeless in one form or another," in *Welfare to What? Part II,* National Coalition for the Homeless, Los Angeles Coalition to End Hunger & Homelessness, on behalf of the National Welfare Monitoring and Advocacy Partnership, Washington, DC, April 19, 2001

WHERE THE HOMELESS LIVE

When faced with high rents and low-housing availability, many poor people become homeless. What happens to them? Where do they live? Research shows that after becoming homeless, many people move around, staying in one place for awhile, then another. The 1996 Urban Institute study shows some basic descriptive information gathered in a point-in-time interview of homeless clients. (See Figure 4.2.) The surveyors asked homeless clients where they had slept on the day before the interview and/or the previous seven days. Many of the clients fell into more than one of the categories, moving from place to place as needs dictated. While 73 percent of the interviewees reported staying in shelters sometime during the previous day or days, 25 percent of the total respondents reported living in three different places in the previous week: shelters, temporary housing, and the streets.

Emergency Housing: Shelters and Transitional Housing

Typically, a homeless shelter provides dormitory-style sleeping accommodations and bathing facilities, with varying services for laundry, telephone calls, and other needs. Residents are often limited in the length of their stays and must leave the shelter during the day

under most circumstances. Transitional housing, on the other hand, is intended to bridge the gap between the shelter or street and permanent housing, with appropriate services to move the homeless into independent living. It may be a room in a hotel or motel, or it may be a subsidized apartment.

According to the U.S. Conference of Mayors (Table 2.2, Chapter 2), the number of demands for emergency shelter beds in 2000 in the 25 major cities surveyed increased overall by an average of 15 percent during the previous year, compared to a 12 percent increase in 1999. Seventy-six percent of the cities reported an increase in demand, compared to 69 percent in 1999.

Shelters have been playing a part in welfare reform. In April 2001 the National Welfare Monitoring and Advocacy Partnership Agency published its findings on the status of former welfare recipients who had been eliminated from the rolls as a result of the welfare reform legislation passed in 1996. (See Figure 4.3.) The study revealed that 44 percent of the respondents were living in a rental unit. Of those in rental units, only 10 percent received subsidized housing. Another 6 percent of those who had been on welfare now owned their own home. The remaining 50 percent of the respondents did not own a home or have an apartment of their own and were either homeless or would be homeless if not for the fact that they were living with relatives. Twenty percent reported that they were staying

TABLE 4.2

Primary nighttime residence of homeless children and youth, 1996–97

State	Shelters	Doubled-Up	Unsheltered	Others	Unknown	Total
Alabama	5816	462	768	-	-	7046
Alaska	853	460	90	-	-	1403
Arizona[1]	-	-	-	-	-	-
Arkansas	2530	6964	1304	516	698	12012
California[2]	46350	60650	13364	28783	-	149147
Colorado[3]	750	1795	-	100	620	3265
Connecticut[4]	3286	-	-	-	-	3286
Delaware[5]	1380	-	-	-	-	1380
Florida[6]	-	-	-	-	-	-
Georgia	12059	835	595	80	135	13704
Hawaii	377	-	237	-	363	600
Idaho[7]	-	-	-	-	-	-
Illinois	2093	15388	383	-	-	17864
Indiana	13500	5400	3200	2200	2700	27000
Iowa	1662	5020	1613	1554	-	9849
Kansas	1778	416	69	65	106	3434
Kentucky	1092	5000	600	-	378	7070
Louisiana	3826	1593	8017	-	200	13636
Maine	3458	-	-	-	-	3458
Maryland[8]	4096	1001	82	8	194	5381
Massachusetts	1671	200	475	492	100	2938
Michigan	28800	7200	1300	4500	1600	43400
Minnesota	2105	-	-	-	-	2105
Mississippi[9]	-	-	-	-	-	-
Missouri	585	2854	476	0	0	3915
Montana	1132	1046	141	141	368	2828
Nebraska	4636	-	1814	-	-	6450
Nevada	28	875	366	421	80	1770
New Hampshire	833	-	-	-	-	833
New Jersey	2079	996	15	6779	5	9874
New Mexico	80	962	54	-	-	1096
New York	23362	2060	-	-	-	25422
North Carolina[10]	-	-	-	-	-	-
North Dakota	98	66	-	-	12	176
Ohio	6984	17460	2910	-	1746	29100
Oklahoma	2987	3758	116	-	-	6861
Oregon	10341	5475	2028	1825	608	20277
Pennsylvania	21693	1500	-	1128	-	24321
Puerto Rico	1147	4365	894	-	-	6406
Rhode Island	1286	53	1	2	289	1631
South Carolina	464	2721	36	481	693	4395
South Dakota	3096	1161	1225	967	0	6449
Tennessee	2223	5992	773	386	290	9664
Texas	29207	88612	-	29274	-	147093
Utah	1490	8012	1385	1818	649	13354
Vermont	434	233	49	47	19	782
Virginia	9108	2137	241	633	905	13024
Washington	8048	-	-	-	-	8048
West Virginia	280	2344	125	930	573	4252
Wisconsin	13371	6685	-	836	-	20892
Wyoming[11]	-	-	-	-	-	-
Totals	**118675**	**138448**	**10073**	**40527**	**6906**	**314449**

[1] No report was submitted.
[2] California reported 69,812 families have been reported as homeless during some portion of the year and have moved to permanent housing.
[3] Number unknown by State.
[4] No source data was available for other categories.
[5] No information was reported.
[6] This data was not collected by the State.
[7] No report was submitted.
[8] Data based on information reported by 17 Local Educational Agencies (LEAs).
[9] This data was not collected by the State.
[10] This data was not collected by the State.
[11] No report was submitted.

SOURCE: "Table 5: Primary Nighttime Residence of Homeless Children and Youth, 1996–97," in *Education for Homeless Children and Youth Program: Report to Congress, Fiscal Year 1997*, United States Department of Education, Washington, DC, 1997

in emergency shelters, while 12 percent were in transitional shelters. (*Welfare to What? Part II,* National Coalition for the Homeless/Los Angeles Coalition to End Hunger & Homelessness/National Welfare Monitoring and Advocacy Partnership, 2001).

Illegal Occupancy

Poor neighborhoods are often full of abandoned buildings. Even the best-intentioned landlords cannot afford to maintain their properties in these areas, not that all of the landlords have the best of intentions. Many have

FIGURE 4.4

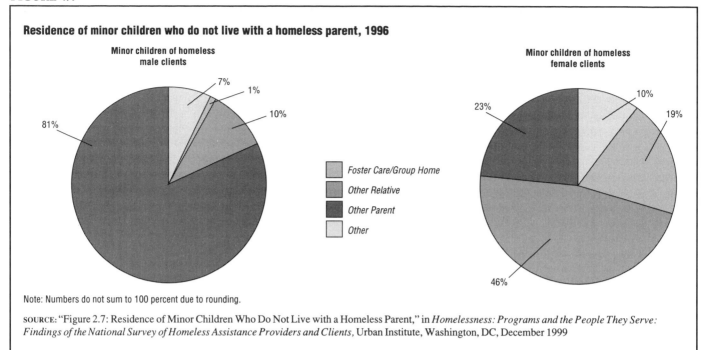

Residence of minor children who do not live with a homeless parent, 1996

Minor children of homeless
male clients

7%
1%
10%
81%

Minor children of homeless
female clients

10%
23%
19%
46%

- Foster Care/Group Home
- Other Relative
- Other Parent
- Other

Note: Numbers do not sum to 100 percent due to rounding.

SOURCE: "Figure 2.7: Residence of Minor Children Who Do Not Live with a Homeless Parent," in *Homelessness: Programs and the People They Serve: Findings of the National Survey of Homeless Assistance Providers and Clients,* Urban Institute, Washington, DC, December 1999

let their buildings deteriorate or have simply walked away, leaving the fate of the building and its residents in the hands of the government. Despite overcrowding and unsafe conditions, many homeless people move into these dilapidated buildings illegally, glad for what shelter they can find. Municipal governments, overwhelmed by long public-housing waiting lists and a lack of funds and personnel, are often unable or unwilling to strictly enforce housing laws, allowing the homeless to become "squatters" rather than forcing them into the streets. Some deliberately turn a blind eye to the problem, knowing they have no better solution for the homeless.

The result is a multitude of housing with deplorable living conditions—tenants bedding down in illegal boiler basements or sharing beds with children or in-laws, bathrooms with strangers. The buildings may have leaks and rot, rusted fire escapes, and rat and roach infestations. Given the alternative, many homeless people feel lucky to be sheltered.

THE RISK OF SQUATTING. These situations can leave the homeless vulnerable to legal remedies or public criticism. In December of 1999, in Worcester, Massachusetts, a homeless couple had taken up residence in an abandoned building. Allegedly, one of them knocked over a candle during an argument, and the building caught fire. The Worcester fire department was called, and six firefighters were killed. The homeless man and woman were each charged with involuntary manslaughter. The public outcry against the homeless couple, and against homeless people in general, reached national proportions. Frustration ran rampant in the ranks of homeless advocates. Most believed the Worces-

ter couple was guilty of nothing more than trying to stay alive. In an Associated Press story dated December 8, 1999, Nicole Witherbee, policy coordinator for the Massachusetts Coalition for the Homeless, reflected the frustration well when she said: "We make laws all the time, they can't panhandle, they can't loiter, we don't have enough shelter beds, so when they go into abandoned buildings it's trespassing. So where is it they're supposed to be?"

Homeless Children

The Department of Education conducted a state-by-state survey of homeless children in school and asked them questions about their life. (*Education for Homeless Children and Youth Program,* United States Department of Education, 1997.) The results show a total of 314,449 homeless children in the 48 reporting states. (See Table 4.2.) The most frequently reported residence for homeless children was in shelters, with 118,675 children nationally staying there each night. The next largest group of homeless children, 138,448, stayed doubled up with others, presumably family or friends. Most distressing for those concerned about the health and well-being of children is that over 10,000 are unsheltered nightly.

When families become homeless, they are subject to frequent moves. This is hard on the children and the solidity of the family unit. Consequently, children of homeless parents are not always accompanying their parents in their efforts at finding shelter. Many families are separated during the hardest times. Parents may ask a family member to care for the child until he or she is settled. Sometimes Children's Services steps in and places the child in foster care until the home life is stable. The children of homeless parents can wind up in any number of living arrangements. Figure 4.4 from the Urban Institute illustrates the residences of those children not living with their homeless parents (*Homeless Programs and the People They Serve, National Survey of Homeless Assistance Providers and Clients,* Urban Institute, 1999).

The Urban Institute results show when the child of a homeless parent is not living with that parent, the gender of the homeless parent greatly affects where they do live. Children with a homeless father are more than three times as likely to live with their mother (81 percent) than children with a homeless mother are to live with their father (23 percent). Children with homeless fathers will stay at a relative's 10 percent of the time, but children with a homeless mother are more than four times as likely (46 percent) to be housed in this manner. It appears that children with a homeless mother are more likely to suffer the loss of both parents than are children with a homeless father.

CHAPTER 5
FEDERAL GOVERNMENT AID FOR THE HOMELESS

In the United States, when there is a problem as widespread as homelessness, many people expect the government to step in. Exactly what the government's role in combating homelessness should be is a hot topic for debate. Some people believe it's the duty of the government to look out for the American citizen in every way. Others point out that government help has all too often been misdirected or inadequate; in some instances, it has even added to the problem, and some feel that people are better served by working things out for themselves.

A TIMELINE OF GOVERNMENT INVOLVEMENT

Since 1860 the federal government has been actively involved with the housing industry, specifically, the low-income housing industry. In 1860 the government called for the first census information on housing—by counting slave dwellings. Twenty years later the U.S. Census focused on the living quarters of the rest of the population, conducting a full housing census. Since then, the federal government has played an increasingly large role in combating housing problems in the United States.

1892—Congress designates $20,000 for a Labor Department study on slum conditions in Baltimore, New York, Chicago, and Philadelphia, the four cities with populations over 200,000 at that time. The study reveals 14 percent of the cities' populations live in slums under crowded conditions and are mostly foreign immigrants. Most spend one-third or more of their income on rent.

1908—President Theodore Roosevelt appoints a Housing Commission to study the problems in American slums; among the suggestions made by the panel are broad federal acquisition of slum properties and direct loans from the federal government to finance the renovation and construction of decent, sanitary housing, which the poor can buy or occupy at low interest rates or rents.

1925—Borrowing and mortgaging properties reach their highest levels ever to that date. The rate of foreclosures also starts to rise, leading to increased homelessness. Although no one knows it at the time, the debts that Americans have run up for their housing will be a major problem in just a few years, when the Great Depression begins.

1929—The stocks trading at the New York Stock Exchange suffer a tremendous crash in prices. The Great Depression has begun.

1932—As many Americans lose their jobs, and failing banks call in their loans, homelessness skyrockets. The Emergency Relief and Construction Act authorizes the Reconstruction Finance Corporation to lend government money to corporations to build housing for low-income families.

1933—The National Industrial Recovery Act allows the Public Works Administration (a government-sponsored work program) to use federal funds for slum clearance, low-cost housing, and subsistence homesteads; close to 40,000 units are produced this year.

1937—The United States Housing Act of 1937 establishes the Public Housing Administration (which will later merge into the Federal Housing Administration [FHA] and the Department of Housing and Urban Development [HUD]) to create low-rent housing programs across the country through the establishment of local public housing agencies.

1938—The National Housing Act Amendments are implemented. They allow the FHA to insure low-income rental projects built for profit.

1940—The U.S. Census, reporting on the first comprehensive survey of the nation's housing stock, shows 18 percent of the housing units need major repairs, 31 percent lack running water, 44 percent have neither a bathtub nor a shower, and 35 percent lack a flush toilet. The worst conditions generally are found in inner-city slums and in the South.

1941—The United States enters World War II (1941–45). The economy surges to meet wartime needs, and millions of young men enter the military. As a result, the Great Depression comes to a close.

1946—The Farmers Home Administration (FmHA) is created under the Department of Agriculture to provide low-income housing assistance in rural areas.

1949—The Housing Act of 1949 sets the goals of "a decent home and a suitable environment" for every family and authorizes an 810,000-unit public housing program over the next six years; Title I creates the Urban Renewal program; Title V creates the basic rural housing program under the FmHA, which puts the federal government directly into the mortgage business.

1961—President Kennedy calls for action to accelerate urban renewal projects, make more mortgage funds available to those seeking housing, and provide decent housing for low-income and minority households. He makes decent housing for all Americans a national objective. Congress passes the Housing Act of 1961, creating a new program for FHA-insured, low-income rental housing. This is the FHA's first direct subsidy program.

1965—Congress establishes the Department of Housing and Urban Development (HUD). Its goal is to create a new rent supplement program for low-income households in private housing.

1968—The Housing and Urban Development Act is passed in response to President Johnson's Message to Congress on Housing and Cities that declares "America's cities are in crisis"; it sets a national housing goal of 26 million new units (6 million are targeted to low- and moderate-income households) over the next 10 years; it provides two new options for low- and moderate-income rent subsidy programs and mortgage insurance for low- and moderate-income families with poor credit histories.

1970—A massive reorganization of federal housing organizations is completed. FHA and HUD are blended under one program, retaining the name of HUD. With the reorganization of HUD, the mission of the FHA has changed to an active advocacy of social policy through targeted support for lower-priced housing and by directing home ownership and rental opportunities to low-income households in inner cities.

1973—President Nixon declares a moratorium on housing and community development assistance, suspending all subsidized housing programs.

1974—The Housing and Community Development Act of 1974 creates a new leased-housing program that includes a certificate (voucher) program, expanding housing choices for low-income tenants and fair-market rent ceilings to

control the cost of the program. The voucher program soon becomes known as Section 8, after the section of the act that established it.

1981—The Housing and Community Development Amendments of 1981 require subsidized tenants to pay up to 30 percent of their income for rent before qualifying for assistance under Section 8 and further targets the Section 8 and public housing programs to limit their benefits to only the neediest households.

1983—The Housing and Urban-Rural Recovery Act of 1983 establishes rental rehabilitation programs and modifies components of the Section 8 program to limit its benefits. Under Section 8, an experimental housing voucher program is established, and new rehabilitation grants and housing development grants are created.

1987—The Stewart B. McKinney Homelessness Assistance Act is passed. This is the first federal act aimed directly at helping the homeless. It establishes new programs and funding for HUD, aimed at helping provide emergency shelter to the homeless and eventually helping secure permanent housing for them.

1989—The HUD Reform Act of 1989 is enacted. Its intent is to clean up HUD and prevent the scandalous misuse of funds that had been plaguing the agency.

1990—The National Affordable Housing Act renews the federal government's commitment to home ownership, tenant-based assistance, and subsidized housing. The Low-Income Housing Preservation and Residential Home Ownership Act demonstrates a federal commitment to permanent preservation of assisted low-income, multi-family housing; the act also repeals the rental rehabilitation grant and the rehabilitation loan program. A special homeless assistance component of the moderate rehabilitation program is retained.

THE MCKINNEY HOMELESS ASSISTANCE ACT

Widespread public outcry over the plight of the homelessness in the early 1980s prompted Congress to pass the Stewart B. McKinney Homeless Assistance Act of 1987. The range and reach of the McKinney Act is broad, having gone through several revisions over the years. Initially the McKinney money went almost exclusively to funding homeless shelters. But times have changed, and the programs have changed with them. The Department of Housing and Urban Development (HUD) is the designated administrator for the majority of the McKinney Act money; housing for the homeless is the target of the bulk of the funds. In the 1990s, largely due to the continued growth in the homeless population, the focus of homeless assistance efforts has been on permanent rather than temporary housing, the theory being that if temporary housing was truly effective, then homelessness would be decreasing.

The HUD/McKinney Continuum of Care Programs

Since the mid-1990s, HUD's homeless programs have been made available through the Continuum of Care approach. In this system, federal funds are channeled through a local or state network or system designed to coordinate efforts to address homelessness in that region. Nearly all of the homeless housing initiatives in the United States (such as shelters, food pantries, housing vouchers, etc.) are eligible for assistance under the auspices of one of four HUD Continuum of Care programs. According to the reports from the U.S. Conference of Mayors survey, 72 percent of the survey cities reported participation in a Continuum of Care and development oversight during the last year (*A Status Report on Hunger and Homelessness in America's Cities,* U.S. Conference of Mayors). The four programs are:

EMERGENCY SHELTER GRANTS PROGRAM (ESG). Often a homeless individual's or family's first encounter with the organized homeless assistance system is at an emergency shelter. Through ESG, the government helps agencies provide the most basic shelter, service, and assessment efforts. Funding is used for direct client relief, through sheltering the individuals and providing financial assistance to help pay utility services, security deposits, or back rent. Shelter administrators also use the funds to meet their own needs, such as the costs of operating the shelters, providing assessment and transitional services to homeless persons, or preventing homelessness. ESG funds can also be used to build or renovate shelters.

SUPPORTIVE HOUSING (DEVELOPMENT) PROGRAM (SHDP). This program helps provide transitional housing for individuals and families, and permanent housing for handicapped homeless persons. The transitional program enables homeless individuals who previously resided in shelters or other temporary residential settings to achieve independent living. The SHDP program is subdivided into two components, transitional housing and permanent housing:

- The Transitional Housing component of SHDP pays for up to 24 months in a transitional housing facility, during which time the clients are encouraged and supported in their efforts to regain permanent housing. Recipient agencies receive advances for housing acquisition, rehabilitation, and, in limited instances, new construction.

- The Permanent Housing component of SHDP provides independent living for homeless individuals with a chronic disability as an alternative to institutionalization. Agencies are required to integrate the housing into a neighborhood setting and to operate a project for at least 10 years (20 years for the earliest projects).

SHELTER PLUS CARE (S+C). This program helps agencies that specifically target the hardest to serve homeless: those with mental and physical disabilities who are living on the street or in shelters. The program provides for rental assistance funded by HUD and other sources. Assistance for projects is available for 10 years; assistance to sponsors and directly to tenants is available for 5 years.

SINGLE ROOM OCCUPANCY (SRO). Single-room-occupancy housing is housing in a dormitory-style building, where each person has his or her own private room but shares kitchens, bathrooms, and lounges. SRO housing is generally the cheapest type of housing available. With the SRO program, the government tries to encourage the establishment and operation of SRO housing. Subsidy payments fund a project for a period of 10 years in the form of rental assistance in amounts equal to the rent, including utilities, minus the portion of rent payable by the tenants.

Evaluating the Continuum of Care Programs

In 1999 the U.S. General Accounting Office (GAO), an investigative body for Congress, evaluated the effectiveness of the HUD programs. The GAO concluded that while the McKinney programs had helped significant numbers of homeless people regain independence and permanent housing, the number of programs and the differences among them create barriers to their efficient use (*Homelessness: Coordination and Evaluation of Programs Are Essential,* GAO, 1999).

Table 5.1 compares some of the requirements among the HUD/McKinney programs, including how funding is delivered, the organizations eligible to apply for funding, the types of activities eligible for funding, the types of services that can be provided, the types of homeless people each program can serve, the time period for which funds are available, and the amount of matching funds required.

A close look at Table 5.1 reveals some of the strengths and limitations of the programs as mentioned by the GAO. For example, the types of funds available for three out of four programs are listed as "competitive grant" programs. This means that agencies and organizations compete for funding. There are deadlines for applying and a pre-established amount of available funding. As a result, some homeless agencies do not get funded because their competitors either apply earlier or have stronger proposals. Another limitation is that all agencies are not eligible for all the programs, even those that apply to their service populations. A nonprofit mental health organization, for example, cannot receive money for a transitional living project for its clients from the program designed to serve mental health clients, Shelter Plus Care. Only state and local governments are eligible for those funds.

FEDERALLY OWNED OR SUBSIDIZED HOUSING

During the years of the Great Depression, when homelessness reached record levels, affordable housing was also in short supply. By the mid-1930s, it became apparent that

TABLE 5.1

Requirements of four Housing and Urban Development (HUD) McKinney programs

Program Requirement	Emergency shelter grants program	Supportive housing program	Shelter plus care program	Single-room occupancy program
Types of funds	Formula grant	Competitive grant	Competitive grant	Competitive grant
Eligible applicants	States Metropolitan cities Urban counties Territories	States Local governments Other governement agencies Private nonprofit organizations Community mental health centers that are public nonprofit organizations	States Local governments Public housing authorities	Public housing authorities Private nonprofit organizations
Eligible program components	Emergency shelter Essential social services	Transitional housing Permanent housing for people with disabilities Supportive services only Safe havens Innovative supportive housing	Tenant based rental assistance Sponsor based rental assistance Project based rental assistance SRO based rental assistance	Single-room occupancy housing
Eligible activities	Renovation/conversion Major rehabilitation Supportive service Operating costs Homelessness prevention activities	Acquisition Rehabilitation New construction Leasing Operating and administrative costs Supportive services	Rental assistance	Rental assistance
Eligible population	Homeless individuals and families People at risk of becoming homeless	Homeless individuals and families for transitional housing and supportive services Disabled homeless individuals for permanent housing Hard-to-reach mentally ill homeless individuals for safe havens	Disabled homeless individuals and their families	Homeless individuals
Initial term of assistance	1 year	Up to 3 years	5 or 10 years	10 years
Matching funds	States: no match for first $100,000 and dollar-for-dollar match for rest of funds Local governments: dollar-for-dollar match for all funds	Dollar-for-dollar match for acquisition, rehabilitation, and new construction grants Operating costs must be shared by 25 percent in the first 2 years and 50 percent in the third year A 25 percent match for supportive service grants No match for grants used for leasing or administrative costs	Dollar-for-dollar match of the federal shelter grant to pay for supportive services	No match required

SOURCE: "Table 1.1: Requirements of Four HUD McKinney Programs," in *Homelessness: Consolidating HUD's McKinney Programs*, General Accounting Office, Washington, DC, May 23, 2000

the private housing market was not meeting the needs of the nation's poorest citizens. The Roosevelt administration responded by passing the Housing Act of 1937, counteracting homelessness with government-funded housing programs. Since that time, the government has continued to use subsidized housing initiatives as a way of moving homeless people from the streets into a higher quality of life, as well as preventing those with low incomes from ending up on the streets in the first place. Government-sponsored low-income housing assistance subsidies are currently provided through one of three methods:

1. Public housing projects—low-income housing units built or renovated with federal money that are owned and managed either directly by the federal government or on its behalf by a local government agency. They are intended for occupancy by low-income households.

2. Tenant-based assistance—federal subsidies granted directly to eligible tenants to cover a portion of their rents.

3. Publicly assisted housing—low-income housing units owned by private landlords who apply for HUD subsidies. Eligible tenants in their units pay a reduced rent, with federal funds covering the rest.

Public Housing Projects

Public housing comes in many sizes, from a single-family home to a high-rise apartment complex. In 2000 HUD reported that there were 1,300,493 public housing units available in 1998, within a total of 14,045 housing projects nationwide. Most of these public housing projects were in neighborhoods with high average poverty rates (28–36 percent of the neighborhood in poverty) and high minority rates (53–59 percent of neighborhood residents). Half of the units had one or fewer bedrooms, 24 percent had two bedrooms, and 26 percent had three or more bedrooms (*A Picture of Subsidized Households 1998,* HUD, 1998, updated April 2001).

PUBLIC HOUSING RESIDENTS. Approximately 1.3 million renters lived in public housing units in 1998. A 1996 HUD study of public housing developments, published in 1999, revealed that all of the developments had residents who were extremely poor, poorly educated, and heavily dependent on welfare programs. Eighty-four percent of the residents in the studied sample group of 23 developments reported income from public assistance. The percentages ranged from a high of 90 percent in an Oakland, California, project to a low of 43 percent in Detroit (which has a large population of elderly residents who receive Social Security.) Only one development, in Charlotte, North Carolina, had a substantial proportion (over 25 percent) of residents who had earned income from a regular job. Also notable is HUD's finding that single women headed the majority of the most impoverished households in public housing developments (*An Historical and Baseline Assessment of HOPE VI,* HUD, August 1999).

PUBLIC HOUSING AGENCIES. Public Housing Agencies (PHAs) are organizations created by local governments to administer HUD's continuum of care housing programs. PHAs work under contract with HUD to develop, own, and manage many of the federally funded public housing developments, as well as other federal programs to assist those who need help paying for housing. For instance, PHAs process individual applications and determine renter eligibility for Section 8 tenant-based certificates and vouchers. Basically, the PHAs decide how low-income housing money will be used in their states, regions, or communities, and HUD provides the funding. In larger urban areas PHAs tend to be city agencies such as the Boston Housing Authority or the Los Angeles Housing Authority. In some less densely populated areas, the state government operates a PHA for most or all of the state.

PUBLIC HOUSING PROBLEMS. Government housing projects have had a problematic history, laden with stories of unsafe living conditions for tenants and fraudulent practices by PHAs. HUD is supposed to monitor the activities of PHAs and ensure that they operate good facilities that meet federal guidelines. Yet HUD has routinely been accused of, and has had to acknowledge, a lack of oversight of housing agencies and low-income housing projects.

In 1990 Congress created the National Commission on Severely Distressed Public Housing to study troubled public housing issues. In its report, released in August 1992, the Commission concluded that severely distressed public housing was a national problem. The Commission reported that 86,000 (or 6 percent) of the nation's public housing units were plagued by crime and deteriorated

physical conditions, in violation of HUD standards. According to the National Housing Institute, five years after the Commission's report, in 1997, HUD still didn't know how much, or which parts, of its public housing inventory met its own "troubled housing" definition, despite the fact that these troubled properties represent a significant portion of the available low-income housing in the United States (J. Atlas and E. Shoshkes, *Saving Affordable Housing, What Community Groups Can Do and What Government Should Do,* National Housing Institute, 1997).

Troubled housing refers to low-income projects that are badly deteriorated, in unsafe neighborhoods, or in danger of being lost to market-rate housing conversion or foreclosure. In an effort to improve their accountability for the conditions of low-income housing, in January 2000 HUD began to implement a new Public Housing Assessment System (PHAS). The PHAS is used to measure the performance of public housing agencies. The four primary PHAS components are:

1. Physical Inspection Indicator—ensures that PHAs meet the minimum standard of being decent, safe, sanitary, and in good repair.

2. Financial Condition Indicator—oversees the finances of PHAs.

3. Management Operations Indicator—evaluates the effectiveness of PHA management methods.

4. Resident Satisfaction and Service Indicator—allows public housing residents to assess PHA performance.

However, a November 2000 GAO report concluded that the new PHA performance assessment system showed no improvement over the old methods, failing to adequately evaluate the performance of PHAs (*Public Housing: HUD Needs Better Information on Housing Agencies' Management Performance,* GAO, 2000). The GAO found that the self-reported data from the PHAs was not verified by HUD and was often inaccurate. For example, a number of agencies certified their housing agency to be standard or high performers but were later found to fit the HUD definition of "troubled."

Of further concern to the GAO was that a PHA's failure to comply with federal housing regulations often went unpunished by HUD. The GAO analysis found that when HUD exercised its powers and punished substandard PHAs, the performance of those PHAs generally improved. Yet most HUD field offices failed to punish poorly performing PHAs.

Revitalizing Housing Projects: HOPE VI

Since the 1970s HUD has funded few new units of public housing. As a result of the 1992 recommendations by the National Commission on Severely Distressed

Public Housing, the HOPE VI Program was developed by HUD to eliminate or revitalize severely distressed public housing. Since privately owned low-income housing has been declining for decades, the HOPE VI program plays an important role in ensuring as much adequate low-income housing as possible is available, thereby helping to reduce homelessness.

The HOPE VI Public Housing Revitalization Program targets housing revitalization in three general areas: physical improvements (including demolition), improvements in management, and providing social and community services to address residents' needs. In a 1999 report, HUD states that, of the developments targeted for revitalization and studied by researchers, the physical conditions of almost one-half of the developments were rated as "poor" or "very poor." Most of the developments targeted for revitalization have serious design flaws. For example, the wooden-frame construction supporting New Orleans' Desire housing complex is rotting because the development is built on a swamp. Other design flaws reported by HUD are poorly designed buildings for housing families, overly small units, and a high number of units per acre. Because of the local and autonomous control of PHAs, there is considerable variation among the developments in the degree to which they are affected by these problems. The HUD study also noted that in many cases the conditions in the surrounding neighborhoods were almost as severe as those in the developments themselves (*An Historical and Baseline Assessment of HOPE VI*, HUD, August 1999).

In a 2001 report, the Urban Institute reported that HOPE VI efforts had resulted in a substantial deconcentration of poverty. Most public housing residents with Section 8 assistance, relocated because of HOPE VI revitalization efforts, have moved to neighborhoods that are less distressed than those they left behind. The report states that the average poverty rate of the residents' neighborhood has dropped from 61 percent in their old neighborhoods to less than half that level (27 percent) in their new neighborhoods. These data pertain only to about 31 percent of all HOPE VI relocatees—those receiving Section 8 assistance. They do not count the 49 percent of the residents who relocated to other public housing developments or the 20 percent who moved to other types of HUD assisted projects or no longer receive HUD assistance.

The 2001 Urban Institute report also notes that racial concentration has been reduced, but not as significantly as poverty concentrations. The minority share of total population in the new (post-relocation) neighborhoods averaged 68 percent, down 20 percent from the 88 percent average in the original neighborhood.

DRAWBACKS OF HOPE VI. HUD's Office of Public Housing Investments (OPHI) is the office that manages HOPE VI projects. The 2001 Urban Institute report was prepared for the OPHI because there is serious concern that in some developments the local PHAs operating HOPE VI projects have lost many original residents in the process of displacement and relocation. The report reveals that negative PHA practices include:

- Failure to involve residents in project planning.
- Failure to inform residents of plans being implemented.
- Aggressive eviction policies.
- Harassment tactics to force residents to move.
- Failure to provide adequate relocation counseling and supportive services.
- Setting standards in order to prevent residents from returning to the development after revitalization.

Many PHAs are now competing for HUD's HOPE VI funding for the demolition and redevelopment of older and deteriorated public housing. However, homeless advocates are concerned that these efforts will not result in increased low-income housing, because as PHAs attempt to revitalize the image of public housing, many units developed under the HOPE VI program are being targeted to moderate-income rather than low-income households.

Tenant-Based Assistance: Section 8 Vouchers

Since its creation in 1974, the Section 8 Housing Choice Voucher program has been the most widely used program for rental assistance in the United States. Program-eligible tenants typically pay 30 percent of their income in rent, and the government covers the difference between this and the rent charged for the unit in the form of a subsidy. The program was created by Congress to allow low-income households more choice in housing and to reduce the concentration of low-income households living in particular neighborhoods, especially in urban areas. Prior to Section 8 vouchers, almost all low-income, subsidized renters lived in large, inner-city, public housing projects. Under the Section 8 tenant-based program, tenants have greater housing choices, since they are able to select housing in communities or neighborhoods based on their own preferences. Section 8 vouchers can be used for public housing, but they are used primarily to subsidize rents in the private market.

QUALIFYING FOR SECTION 8 VOUCHERS. In the Section 8 program, low-income families apply to the PHA for rent subsidy vouchers. Eligibility is based on the total annual gross income and family size. Each PHA sets its own standards within a set of guidelines established by HUD. Generally, the family's income may not exceed 50 percent of the median income for the area in which they choose to live. Median income levels are published by HUD and vary by location.

Assuming that a family qualifies for a Section 8 subsidy, they still have to find an apartment that meets the program's requirements. The Section 8 program will only help to pay for apartments where the rent is at or below the fair market rent (FMR). The FMR is an amount that has been determined by HUD to be a fair price for rental housing, including utilities. The FMR varies from one region to another, just as rental prices do. HUD determines the FMR by studying how much rent was paid by people who had found new apartments in the past 15 months and taking the 40th percentile of those rents. This means that the FMR is set to an amount where 40 percent of the people paid less than the FMR, and 60 percent paid more than the FMR. HUD uses the 40th percentile because it feels that if it went lower, then people in the program would not have enough choices about where to live. Yet it cannot go higher, since that would mean helping people to pay for relatively expensive, better-than-average rental housing, which is not the purpose of the program. Section 8 is intended to help as many people as possible get a decent place to live, a goal it cannot accomplish if it spends too much money on too few people living in particularly nice apartments.

The FMR may sound relatively low, but there are a great many people in America who could not afford to pay it without Section 8 assistance. The federal government believes that no more than 30 percent of a family's income should go towards housing and utilities. Yet in order to afford the median Fair Market Rent for a two-bedroom rental unit in the United States, without spending more than 30 percent of his or her income on it, a minimum wage worker would have to work hundreds of hours a week. Data provided by the National Low Income Housing Coalition (NLIHC) shows wage/rent comparisons of the 10 least affordable states, using three different methods to illustrate the disparity between wages and rents. (See Table 5.2.) For example, in Maryland a worker earning minimum wage would have to work the equivalent of 103 hours per week in order to afford the median Fair Market Rent for a two-bedroom rental unit.

In other areas of the country, housing is even less affordable to low-wage workers. To afford a two-bedroom unit in New York, while working at the minimum wage, a household must generate 123 hours of work per week for the median rent. In Virginia, more than half the renters in the state cannot afford a two-bedroom apartment. Table 5.3 shows the hourly wage needed in the ten least affordable states in order to afford the two-bedroom FMR.

HOW EFFECTIVE IS SECTION 8? Advocates agree that when the Section 8 Housing Choice Voucher program works as designed, it enables low-income households access to adequate housing and helps provide a better quality of life. However, there are some significant factors that inhibit the success of program recipients in obtaining decent housing. For one, there is usually a very long waiting list for Section 8 certificates and vouchers because the

TABLE 5.2

Least affordable states

Estimated percent of renters unable to afford 2 bedrooms at fair market rent

Virginia	53%
New York	52%
Rhode Island	51%
Vermont	50%
Maine	48%
Pennsylvania	47%
Montana	47%
Massachusetts	45%
New Hampshire	45%
New Jersey	45%

Estimated percent of federal minimum wage needed to afford 2 bedrooms at fair market rent

Hawaii	330%
New Jersey	309%
New York	308%
District of Columbia	306%
Massachusetts	296%
Alaska	291%
California	289%
Connecticut	286%
Maryland	257%
Nevada	257%

Estimated hours/week needed to work at federal minimum wage to afford 2 bedrooms at fair market rent

Hawaii	132
New Jersey	123
New York	123
District of Columbia	122
Massachusetts	119
Alaska	116
California	116
Connecticut	114
Maryland	103
Nevada	103

SOURCE: "Least Affordable States (Total Population)," in *Out of Reach, September 1999: The Gap Between Housing Costs and Income of Poor People in the United States*, National Low Income Housing Coalition, Washington, DC, September 1999.

TABLE 5.3

Least affordable metropolitan statistical areas (MSA)

MSA	Housing wage for two bedrooms at fair market rent
San Francisco, CA	$28.06
San Jose, CA	$25.15
Stamford-Norwalk, CT	$22.62
Nassau-Suffolk, NY	$22.56
Westchester County, NY	$22.00
Santa Cruz-Watsonville, CA	$20.98
Oakland, CA	$18.94
Orange County, CA	$18.85
Boston, MA-NH	$18.83

SOURCE: "Least Affordable Metropolitan Statistical Areas (MSAs)," in *Out of Reach, September 2000: The Growing Gap Between Housing Costs and Income of Poor People in the United States*, National Low Income Housing Coalition, Washington, DC, September 2000.

demand for housing assistance often exceeds the available resources. Many PHAs close their Section 8 waiting lists because they know that they have more applicants than they will be able to help. Housing advocates have also noted that Section 8 programs are subject to discrimination, since each PHA is autonomous and can establish its own criteria to determine an applicant's place on a waiting list. For example, a PHA may decide that priority be given to families with children under five years old. Families that meet this qualification can then move ahead of others who may have been on the list for years. In 1999 the Department of Housing and Urban Development reported that the total number of households on Section 8 waiting lists was approximately one million, with an average waiting time of 28 months. Keep in mind that this does not include the large number of qualified people who were not allowed to put their names on the waiting list at all (*Waiting in Vain: An Update on America's Rental Housing Crisis,* HUD, Washington, D.C., 1999).

Besides long waiting lists, Section 8 participants must contend with other obstacles in their efforts to obtain safe, affordable housing. One of the most frequent complaints of voucher holders is that the only types of available housing are often sub-standard. A 1997 report on Section 8-assisted properties released by the National Housing Institute revealed that the physical conditions of subsidized units ranged from very good to very poor (J. Atlas and E. Shoshkes, *Saving Affordable Housing, What Community Groups Can Do and What Government Should Do,* National Housing Institute, 1997). The NHI report concluded that the properties in good physical condition—where landlords are compliant with HUD regulations—demonstrate the effectiveness of the Section 8 program. Unfortunately, the study found disturbing living conditions in many subsidized properties that were in clear violation of HUD housing quality standards. Some of the more frequently reported violations that Section 8 families were compelled to live with included:

- Leaking toilets and sinks.

- Exposed electrical wiring.

- Holes in walls and ceilings.

- Broken air conditioners and smoke detectors.

- Damaged and missing kitchen cabinets.

- Roach and rat infestation.

- Landlords who collected higher rents than did landlords of well-maintained apartments in the same area.

Publicly Assisted, Privately Owned Rental Housing

Beginning in the early 1960s, Congress created a number of programs that encouraged the development of privately owned affordable housing. This was a move away from public housing and toward public/private partnerships where the federal government would provide incentives to private developers to keep all or some of their units in multifamily developments affordable to low-income people. In 1998 HUD reported that almost 1.4 million subsidized, privately-owned housing units were available in the United States.

ENTICEMENTS FOR OWNERS/DEVELOPERS. Developers and owners profit from government subsidies in two ways: (1) they are given mortgage incentives, lucrative annual tax breaks, and grants for renovation and improvement in exchange for designating their units as low-income; and (2) their low-income tenants' payments are subsidized and guaranteed by the federal government.

Federal housing assistance expenditures rose dramatically from 1977 to 2001. The primary payments went to developers to maintain and operate subsidized housing units. This increase amounted to an average of 349 percent over the 24-year period, making housing assistance spending among the very few domestic programs that have grown significantly over the last two decades. Only health care programs—Medicaid rose by 450 percent, and Medicare by 396 percent—have had a higher rate of increase. Figure 5.1 shows the trends in federal housing spending from 1977, projected through 2005. In inflation-adjusted terms, 1977 spending totaled $23.2 billion. By 2001 expenditures were four times as high as in 1977, at $115.1 billion, and are expected to rise to $122.5 billion by 2005.

AN ENDANGERED SUPPLY OF PUBLICLY ASSISTED HOUSING. Initially, the system called for private housing owners and developers to enter into 10- to 15-year contracts with HUD. In exchange for providing low-income housing units, HUD gave them financial support and benefits from the government. Later the contract periods were reduced to five years and, by 2001, to one year. This reduction in the length of contract periods has led to some significant changes in privately owned, low-income housing. When their contracts expire, landlords with subsidized low-income units may opt not to continue in the publicly subsidized market and instead try to compete for higher rents in the regular market. Landlords with properties in high rent areas and those who have benefited from extensive renovation to their properties on the government's tab are the most likely to opt out and to take advantage of the higher market rents.

While the owners and developers received government subsidies to build or renovate their properties for low-income use, there is no penalty for prepayment or conversion to competitive market housing once the contract has expired. Harvard University's Joint Center for Housing Studies reports that by the end of 1999 some 90,000 low-income units had been lost because of mortgage prepayments or opt-outs. They predict that if the current trend continues, by 2004 as many as 180,000 units may also opt out after their contracts expire. If rent increases continue to outpace inflation, the number of lost low-income housing units may go even higher (*The State*

FIGURE 5.1

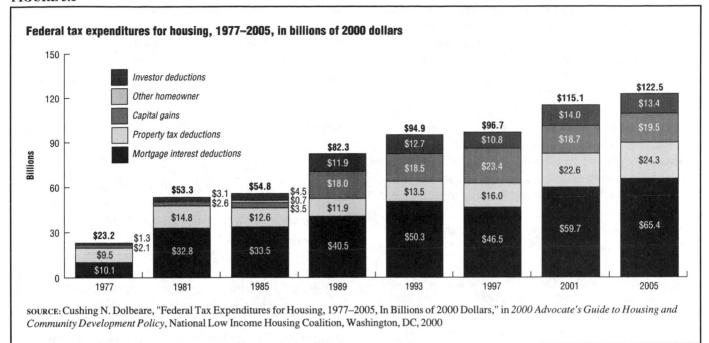

Federal tax expenditures for housing, 1977–2005, in billions of 2000 dollars

SOURCE: Cushing N. Dolbeare, "Federal Tax Expenditures for Housing, 1977–2005, In Billions of 2000 Dollars," in *2000 Advocate's Guide to Housing and Community Development Policy*, National Low Income Housing Coalition, Washington, DC, 2000

of the Nation's Housing: 2000, Joint Center for Housing Studies, June 2000).

INCREASING THE AMOUNT OF AFFORDABLE HOUSING: THE CONSOLIDATED PLAN

Since private low-income rental units are in short supply, new federal initiatives have begun to appear. The Consolidated Plan is a HUD-administered plan to allow states and some local government the ability to increase affordable housing on their own. The Consolidated Plan uses four HUD programs administered by state and local housing officials and is approved by HUD each year. One of these programs, the Emergency Shelter Grant Program, is part of the Continuum of Care programs for the homeless. The other three HUD Consolidated Plan programs arc:

• HOME Revitalization Program.

• Community Development Block Grant Program.

• Housing Opportunities for People with AIDS Program.

HOME Program

The HOME program is a formula grant of federal housing funds to states and local jurisdictions. All housing developed with HOME funds must serve low- and very low-income individuals and families. For rental housing, at least 90 percent of HOME funds must benefit families whose incomes are at or below 60 percent of area median income; the remaining 10 percent must benefit families with incomes at or below 80 percent of area median income. HOME funds can be used for the following:

• Rental housing production and rehabilitation loans and grants.

• First-time homebuyer assistance.

• Rehabilitation loans for homeowners.

• Tenant-based rental assistance (2-year renewable contracts).

Community Development Block Grant

The Community Development Block Grant (CDBG) program is a federal grant, typically provided to states and municipalities with populations over 50,000 and urban counties with populations over 200,000. At least 70 percent of CDBG funds must be used to benefit low- and moderate-income people by providing decent housing and a suitable living environment and by expanding economic opportunities.

Housing for People with AIDS

The Housing Opportunities for People with AIDS program (HOPWA) is a HUD program that funds housing and services for people with AIDS. It is available as a block grant to states and larger metropolitan areas based on the incidence of AIDS in these areas. Eligible activities under the program include housing information and coordination services, homeless prevention activities, project-based or tenant-based rental assistance, and supportive services. Recently, funding for this program was expanded in order to help communities increase low-income housing through the HUD Consolidated Plan.

OTHER GOVERNMENT HOUSING PROGRAMS

The McKinney Act Continuum of Care programs, the Consolidated Plan programs, and the federal government's public housing and housing subsidy programs are the largest and most significant sources of government aid to the homeless. The Department of Housing and Urban Development (HUD) and other government agencies also have many smaller programs to address particular needs.

Low Income Housing Tax Credit (LIHTC)

The federal government initiated the LIHTC program in 1986 in order to create incentives for investment in low-income housing development by giving federal tax credits to investors in affordable low-income housing. Figure 5.1 shows that for fiscal year 2001, investor deductions are at $14 billion, tripling in size from the preprogram (1985) level of $4.5 billion. Investors receive benefits not only for the year of the investment expenditure, but continue to receive a federal tax credit over a 10-year term. The program allows for a developer to designate only 20 percent or 40 percent (depending on the amount of expected rent) of the subsidized units for low-income renters. The rest can be rented at competitive market values. HUD warns interested developers that the program is very competitive.

Federal Home Loan Bank

Federal law requires each of the twelve District Federal Home Loan Banks to establish an Affordable Housing Program (AHP). Member banks then provide grants and below-market loans to organizations for the purchase, construction, and/or rehabilitation of rental housing. Only 20 percent of the units created with these funds must be occupied and affordable to very low-income households.

In addition, the Federal Home Loan Bank offers a loan program called the Community Investment Program (CIP). This provides long-term funding at fixed rates to develop rental housing or finance first-time home purchases for families and individuals with incomes up to 115 percent of the area's median income. This means that middle-income people can build or buy homes using these funds, but the expenses are considered part of the low-income housing assistance budget.

Rural Housing Programs

The Rural Housing Programs are administered by the U.S. Department of Agriculture and make federal money available in an effort to increase both the amount and the quality of housing in rural areas of the country. Rural areas are places and towns with a population of 50,000 or less. Eligibility for rural housing programs is similar to that of subsidized urban programs. The requirements vary from region to region, and applicants must meet minimum and maximum income guidelines. The subsidies come in the form of grants or low-interest loans to repair substandard housing, subsidized mortgages for low-income home ownership, and grants to cover down payment and purchasing costs of low-income homes.

Housing advocates agree that the significant incidence of housing problems in rural areas is often overlooked. In 1997 about one in ten rural owners and one in five rural renters spent more than half their incomes for housing. Yet only 17 percent of very low-income rural renters receive housing subsidies, compared with 28 percent of very low-income urban renters. Roughly a third of rural very low-income owners and an even larger share of very low-income renters faced high cost burdens, particularly in the Northeast. Rural households are also more likely than urban families to live in severely inadequate housing.

Despite this, federal funding for loans and grants specifically targeted to rural households has been reduced dramatically since the 1960s. In addition, assistance has shifted from direct loans providing deeply subsidized assistance to guaranteed loans serving rural residents with higher incomes. As a result, progress in addressing very low-income housing needs in rural areas depends increasingly on rental tax credits and programs provided by HUD.

Projects for Transition from Homelessness (PATH)

This federally funded program is administered by the federal Center for Mental Health Services through grants to state mental health agencies. These state agencies provide PATH funded services to homeless people with mental illness primarily through local or regional mental health service providers. PATH funds can be used for outreach, screening, diagnostic treatment, habilitation, rehabilitation, community mental health services, case management, supportive and supervisory services in residential settings, and other housing-related services.

Education for Homeless Children and Youth

In response to reports that over 50 percent of homeless children were not attending school regularly, Congress enacted the McKinney Education for Homeless Children and Youth (EHCY) program in 1987. The program ensures that homeless children and youth have equal access to the same free, appropriate education, including preschool education, provided to other children. EHCY also allows for funding for state and local school districts to implement the law. The projects provide transportation, transfer of school records, immunization, referrals, school supplies, clothing, and tutoring.

Unaccompanied Youth Services

The Runaway and Homeless Youth Program, administered by the Department of Health and Human Services, provides financial assistance to community-based crisis and referral centers that serve runaway and homeless youth and their families. These centers try to resolve family differences, strengthen family relationships, encourage stable living conditions for young people, and help juveniles decide on constructive courses of action to resolve their problems.

CHAPTER 6

THE LAW, THE COURTS, AND THE HOMELESS

The legal rights of homeless people have been an issue since homelessness became a part of society. There are questions as to whether or not they are disenfranchised (without legal and political rights). While no American who is not in prison or military service ever loses his or her legal rights, in practice the rights of the homeless are not as well protected as those of other people. American society is dominated by those who have homes and is oriented to meet their needs and rights. When the homeless come into conflict with these needs and rights, they rarely come out on top. It is not uncommon for homelessness to be "criminalized" by officials in a region, that is, homeless people have been imprisoned, removed, or interfered with because they were living or loitering in public areas. In other cases, attempts to place homeless and low-income persons in neighborhood housing have met with strenuous political objection and legal action from residents of the neighborhood.

While the federal government has passed many laws on or related to homelessness, it is at the community level that most homelessness measures have been enacted through the years, either against the homeless or on their behalf. These local laws and ordinances often have more impact on the homeless in the region they cover than federal laws do, since these local laws often directly regulate their behavior. Sometimes the more restrictive of these laws are challenged in federal court as violating the rights of the homeless people they seek to regulate, assuming that the homeless people in question can find the legal help to pursue such a claim.

ANTIHOMELESS ORDINANCES

Not in My Backyard (NIMBY)

Many people fear that putting anything in their neighborhood that might attract the homeless or the poor will cause their neighborhood to deteriorate, although there is no indication that this actually happens. Still, because of

these fears, local governments often use zoning requirements to block the establishment of group-living homes and shelters for the homeless in all or part of their city. Zoning requirements are local laws regulating what kinds of buildings can be placed in different parts of a city. This is often called the "Not In My Backyard" (NIMBY) effect, since the people in the neighborhoods are essentially saying that they do not want to have services for the homeless near them, even if they do not oppose them in general.

In 1997 the City of Springfield, Missouri, passed a zoning ordinance that is typical of the NIMBY effect. The ordinance imposed new restrictions on the operation of emergency and transitional shelters and soup kitchens. No such facility was allowed to be located within two thousand feet of another similar facility. Among other restrictions, the ordinance limits the capacity of emergency shelters to 50 beds, prohibits shelters from serving meals to nonshelter residents unless the shelter obtains city authorization, and requires shelters to have at least one off-street parking space for every three beds. The overall effect was to keep services for the homeless small and scattered, with none of them able to provide all of the needs of a homeless person at once.

CRIMINALIZING THE HOMELESS LIFE. Homeless people live in and move about public spaces, and many Americans feel society has a right to control or regulate what homeless people may do in those shared spaces. A city or town may introduce local ordinances or policies designed to restrict homeless activities, remove their belongings, or destroy their nontraditional living places. In many cities, municipal use of criminal sanctions to protect public spaces have come into conflict with efforts by civil rights and homeless advocates to prevent the criminalization of the homeless.

There are also some new approaches. Several cities have proposed or created community courts specifically

TABLE 6.1

Prohibited conduct in selected cities

City	Vagrancy: Closure of particular public places	Vagrancy: Obstruction of sidewalks/public places	Loitering/loafing in particular public places	Loitering/loafing/vagrancy city-wide	Sitting/lying: Sitting or lying down in particular public places	Sleeping/camping: Camping in particular public places	Sleeping/camping: Camping in public city-wide	Sleeping/camping: Sleeping in particular public places	Sleeping/camping: Sleeping in public city-wide	Begging: "Aggressive" panhandling	Begging: Begging in particular public places	Begging: Begging in public places city-wide
New York, NY	X	X			X	X				X	X	
Los Angeles, CA	X	X	X		X	X				X	X	
Chicago, IL	X			X				X		X	X	
Houston, TX	X					X				X		
Philadelphia, PA		X	X		X			X	X	X	X	
San Diego, CA		X	X			X	X	X	X	X		
Dallas, TX	X	X	X							X		
Phoenix, AZ			X									
Detroit, MI												
San Antonio, TX		X			X	X		X			X	X
San Jose, CA		X									X	X
Indianapolis, IN		X		X				X		X	X	
San Francisco, CA	X	X	X						X	X	X	X
Baltimore, MD			X			X					X	
Jacksonville, FL		X	X								X	
Columbus, OH	X[2]	X			X[2]	X[2]	X	X[2]		X		
Milwaukee, WI	X[2]			X						X[2]	X	
Memphis, TN	X				X	X			X	X		
Washington, DC		X	X							X	X	
Boston, MA	X	X				X				X		
El Paso, TX	X	X				X					X	
Seattle, WA	X	X					X		X		X	X
Cleveland, OH	X	X	X						X		X	X
Nashville, TN	X		X			X		X		X	X	
Austin, TX												
New Orleans, LA												
Denver, CO	X					X		X				X
Fort Worth, TX	X	X									X	X
Oklahoma City, OK	X	X					X				X	
Portland, OR	X	X			X	X	X					
Long Beach, CA		X			X					X		
Kansas City, MO		X			X						X	
Virginia Beach, VA		X							X			X
Charlotte, NC		X			X			X			X	
Tucson, AZ	X	X				X						
Albuquerque, NM										X	X	
Atlanta, GA	X	X	X				X	X		X		
St. Louis, MO	X	X		X						X		
Sacramento, CA	X		X	X		X	X			X		
Fresno, CA		X	X			X				X		

TABLE 6.1

Prohibited conduct in selected cities [CONTINUED]

	Begging			Sleeping/camping				Sitting/lying	Loitering/loafing		Vagrancy	
	Begging in public places city-wide	Begging in particular public places	"Aggressive" panhandling	Sleeping in public city-wide	Sleeping in particular public places	Camping in public city-wide	Camping in particular public places	Sitting or lying down in particular public places	Loitering/loafing/ vagrancy city-wide	Loitering/loafing in particular public places	Obstruction of sidewalks/ public places	Closure of particular public places
Tulsa, OK		X				X						X
Oakland, CA			X		X	X				X	X	
Honolulu, HI							X					X
Miami, FL³												
Pittsburgh, PA		X	X				X				X	X
Cincinnati, OH		X	X								X	X
Minneapolis, MN	X						X			X	X	X
Omaha, NE	X					X						
Toledo, OH	X				X					X	X	X
Buffalo, NY	X				X						X	X

*X Denotes existence of current city ordinance. Information obtained from office of city clerk or city attorney in each city, local library, and the Internet. Does not include state laws that impose similar prohibitions on conduct or local legislation currently pending.

¹Null and void after December 31, 1998.

²Denotes county ordinance.

³Information not available.

SOURCE: "Prohibited Conduct," in *Out of Sight—Out of Mind? — A Report on Anti-Homeless Laws, Litigation and Alternatives in 50 United States Cities*, National Law Center on Homelessness and Poverty, Washington, DC, 1999 to handle "public nuisance" crimes. Other cities have implemented plans to privatize public property as a way of restricting homeless people's access to certain areas. The National Law Center on Homelessness and Poverty studied the 50 largest cities in the United States and found that a growing number of cities are enacting laws against living in public (Table 6.1). Among cities surveyed, 86 percent have ordinances that prohibit or restrict begging, up from 77 percent in 1996. In addition, 73 percent of the cities have ordinances prohibiting or restricting sleeping and/or camping.

According to the study results, loitering is the least reported punishable offensive; only four cities prohibit it. Eleven cities have laws against sleeping in a public place, while more than three times that many (34) prohibit obstructing the sidewalk or other public places. Many cities have addressed the presence of homelessness by conducting "police sweeps" to remove the homeless from public view. The homeless are either jailed or transported to suburban or rural areas, much like homeless people in colonial America were.

Many cities enact special laws directed specifically at the homeless. People who are homeless sometimes rest at bus stops or on sidewalks. Tucson, Arizona, has made it unlawful to be at a bus stop more than 30 minutes, and Seattle, Washington, arrests people for sitting on the sidewalk. Some laws ban placing baggage down on the sidewalks, others prohibit storing property in doorways. In many places, it is illegal to sleep or camp in a park. New York City's Mayor Giuliani, in pursuit of a "quality of life" agenda during the 1990s, upholds strictly enforcing laws against sleeping in subways and jumping turnstiles. In 2001 violators, who once were ticketed, are now jailed.

Reminiscent of the force used against striking coal miners at the turn of the 20th century and the homeless and poor World War I veterans who marched on Washington during the Great Depression, violence and force has often been used to deal with the "homeless problem." In 1995 the New York City police used an armored personnel carrier and riot gear to retake two East Village tenements from a group of squatters who had resisted city efforts for nine months. Homeless people had occupied the city-owned buildings for as long as a decade and claimed that their continuous use of the buildings without the formal objection of the city gave them rights to the building, under a legal principle known as "adverse possession."

In Atlanta, nine thousand homeless people were arrested just prior to the 1996 Olympic Games for violating "quality-of-life laws," which make sleeping, lying, or even sitting in public an offense punishable by jail. And in San Francisco, the city confiscates shopping carts that homeless people use to carry their belongings.

The Rationale for Restrictive Laws

Local officials often restrict homeless people's use of public space to protect public health and safety—either of the general public, the homeless themselves, or both. Dangers to the public have included tripping over people and objects on sidewalks, intimidation of passersby caused by aggressive begging, and the spreading of diseases. Many people believe the very presence of the homeless is unsightly, and their removal would improve the appearance of public spaces. Other laws are based on the need to prevent crime. Mayor Giuliani's campaign is based on the "broken windows" theory of criminologists James Q. Wilson and George Kelling (*Atlantic Monthly*, March 1982). Their theory argues that allowing indications of disorder, such as a broken window, or street people, to remain unaddressed shows a loss of public order and control, as well as apathy in a neighborhood, which breeds more serious criminal activity. Therefore, keeping a city neat and orderly should help to prevent crime.

All of these are legitimate concerns to at least some degree. The problem is that, rather than try to eliminate or reduce homelessness by helping the homeless find housing and jobs, most local laws try to change the behavior of the homeless by punishing them. They target the homeless with legal action if they do not change their behavior, ignoring the fact they would gladly stop living in the streets and panhandling if they had any feasible alternatives. While these laws may be effective, in the sense that the shanties may be gone, and homeless people no longer bed down in subway tunnels or doorways where they are in effect, the people haven't disappeared. They have simply been forced to move to a different part of town, or hide, or else they have been imprisoned. Furthermore, many of these laws end up challenged in court as violating the legal rights of the homeless people they target.

AN ARGUMENT AGAINST CRIMINALIZATION AS PUBLIC POLICY. According to Maria Foscarinis, in "Downward Spiral: Homelessness and its Criminalization" (*Yale Law & Policy Review*, Vol. 14, No. 1, 1996), criminalization of the homeless is poor public policy for several reasons:

- It may be constitutionally unsound, especially in cities that are unable to offer adequate resources to their homeless residents.

- It leads to legal challenges, which may take years to resolve, regardless of outcome.

- Legal battles are costly and will deplete already scarce municipal resources that could be used on solutions to homelessness.

- Criminalization responses do not reflect public sentiment, but rather the will of a vocal, politically influential minority.

- Criminalization fosters divisiveness, pitting "us" (the housed) against "them" (the homeless).

- Like emergency relief, criminalization addresses the visible symptom of homelessness—the presence of homeless people in public space—and neglects the true causes of homelessness.

- Finally there is the fact that, in the long-term, criminalization does not and cannot work. Like all humans, homeless people must eat, sleep, and occupy space. If they are prohibited from occupying one area, they must go somewhere else.

As an alternative to criminalization, Foscarinis suggests the following:

- Police advocacy programs, in which "sweeps" are replaced by outreach units—officers assigned to go out, with service providers, to homeless people to refer them to necessary services. Unless criminal activity is involved, the police remain in the background to provide security, and the presence of service providers prevents police from being too heavy handed or harassing.

- Standing committees composed of homeless people, advocates, a police captain, and a representative of the city government to respond to complaints about "camping" of homeless residents. The committee outreach team attempts to make alternative arrangements for the homeless. The police act only if criminal activity is involved, or if homeless people refuse alternative arrangements.

- Day-labor centers—buildings where homeless people can meet with employers to get jobs.

- One-stop access centers, which offer medical services, mental health services, social services, and job training at one location.

CONSTITUTIONAL RIGHTS

The U.S. Constitution and its amendments, especially the Bill of Rights, guarantee certain freedoms and rights to all citizens of the United States, including the homeless. Public place restrictions have often been challenged in court as unconstitutional, specifically as they have been applied to homeless people. Sometimes a city ordinance will be declared unconstitutional; at other times, the court may find that there are special circumstances that allow the ordinance to stand. There are numerous ways in which ordinances on the homeless can violate their rights. Many court challenges claim that the law in question is unconstitutionally broad or vague. Others claim that a particular law denies the homeless equal protection under the law or violates their right to due process, as guaranteed by the Fifth and Fourteenth Amendments. There have also been cases based on a person's right to travel, and others that claimed restrictions on the homeless constituted "cruel

and unusual punishment," which is prohibited by the Eighth Amendment.

Testing the Laws in Court

Some court cases test the law through civil suits and others "try" the law by appealing a conviction in a criminal case. Many advocates for the homeless, or the homeless themselves, have challenged laws that they felt infringed on the rights of homeless people.

USING LIBRARIES. Richard Kreimer, a homeless man in Morristown, New Jersey, often visited the Joint Free Library of Morristown to read or just to sit and think. Because he was homeless, he had little access to television or newspapers and relied on the library for news. The library personnel, however, objected to his presence. They claimed his behavior was disruptive, and his body odor so offensive that it kept patrons from using some of the areas of the library. After the librarians documented the problems for a period of time, the Library Board of Trustees passed a Library Patron Policy that allowed librarians to ask people to leave if their hygiene was unacceptable to community norms, along with other restrictions.

In 1990 Kreimer filed suit in the Federal District Court for New Jersey against the library, the Board of Directors, the Morristown Bureau of Police, and other library and municipal officials. The suit alleged that the policy rules were "overbroad" (that is, they failed to specify what actions would be objectionable), "vague," and a violation of Kreimer's First Amendment right of access to information and his Fourteenth Amendment rights of equal protection and due process, as well as his rights under the New Jersey Constitution.

The district court upheld Kreimer's complaint that the policy violated his First and Fourteenth Amendment rights. The library appealed the decision to the Court of Appeals, and the court reversed the decision, validating the library's policy, finding that a library, by its very nature, cannot support all First Amendment activities, such as speech-making and interactive debate. Therefore, a library is a "limited public forum," and the rules of the Morristown Library were appropriate to its limited functions of reading, studying, and using library materials (*Kreimer v. Bureau of Police for Morristown*, 958 F.2d 1242 [3rd Cir. 1992]).

LOITERING OR WANDERING. In the 1980s the City of Miami, Florida, had a practice of "sweeping" homeless persons from the areas in which the Orange Bowl Parade and other related activities were held. Homeless persons claimed that the police routinely manhandled them, arrested them, and destroyed their property, all for little or no provocation other than living in public areas.

Learning in 1988 that the city planned once again to clear the areas, the Miami Chapter of the American Civil

Liberties Union (ACLU) and law professors of the University of Miami filed a request for a preliminary injunction (a ruling forbidding the continuation of the practice) and a federal class action civil rights lawsuit against Miami. They named three homeless persons, Michael Pottinger, Peter Carter, and Berry Young as representative plaintiffs. (A class action suit is one in which one or several people sue on behalf of themselves and a much larger group that also has the same grounds for suit.)

The court ruled that the city's practice of arresting the homeless for activities such as sleeping, standing, and assembling in public places was in violation of the Eighth Amendment's ban against punishment based on status. (Only the homeless were being arrested.) Furthermore, the court found the police practices of taking or destroying the property of the homeless to be in violation of Fourth and Fifth Amendment rights of freedom from unreasonable seizure and confiscation of property. In addition, the ordinances under which the police arrested the homeless were unconstitutionally overbroad.

LIVING IN AN ENCAMPMENT. In 1996 advocates for the homeless sought an injunction against a Tucson resolution barring homeless encampments from city-owned property on Eighth Amendment and Equal Protection grounds. The court, in *Davidson v. City of Tucson* (924 F. Supp.989), held the plaintiffs did not have standing to raise a cruel and unusual punishment claim, as they had not been convicted of a crime, and no one had been arrested under the ordinance. The Equal Protection claim failed because the court did not consider homeless people a suspect class, and the right to travel does not include the right to ignore trespass laws or remain on property without regard to ownership.

SITTING OR LYING ON THE SIDEWALK. In 1995 homeless persons challenged Cincinnati, Ohio, ordinances prohibiting sitting or lying on sidewalks and solicitation on First and Fourteenth Amendment grounds. In 1998, in *Clark v. Cincinnati* (No. 1-95-448, S.D. Ohio, October 25, 1995), determining that the ordinances likely infringed on the plaintiffs' First Amendment right to freedom of speech, the U.S. District Court issued a preliminary injunction to stop the city from enforcing the ordinances, except for the specific provision of the sidewalk ordinance that prohibited lying down.

LOITERING IN A TRAIN STATION. In 1995 plaintiffs challenged Amtrak's policy of arresting or ejecting persons who appeared to be homeless or loitering in Penn Station in New York City, even though the individuals were not apparently committing crimes. The district court, in *Streetwatch v. National R.R. Passenger Corp.* (875 F. Supp. 1055), issued a preliminary injunction prohibiting Amtrak from continuing the practice, finding that Amtrak's rules of conduct were vague, and that their enforcement impinged on plaintiffs' rights to freedom of movement and due process.

PANHANDLING. In 1996 seven homeless persons filed suit in federal court one month before the opening of the Olympic games in Atlanta, Georgia, challenging Atlanta's ordinances against panhandling and loitering on city streets. The district court, in *Atchison v. Atlanta* (No 1:96-CV-1430), issued a preliminary injunction against enforcement of the ordinances, stating the ordinances were "unconstitutionally vague" but rejecting the plaintiffs' claim that police actions were harassment. Before an appeal was heard, the case was settled, with the city agreeing to redraft the panhandling and parking lot ordinances and require "sensitivity" training for its police officers.

ZONING THE HOMELESS OUT OF DOWNTOWN. A homeless man sought an injunction, damages, and relief against the city of Tucson and the city police for "zoning" homeless people, which restricted them from the downtown areas, charging them with misdemeanors. The zone restrictions placed on the plaintiff included a two-mile square area covering most of downtown Tucson, an area including state, local, and federal courts, voter registration facilities, a soup kitchen, places of worship, and many social and transportation agencies.

The plaintiff argued that such restrictions violated his constitutional right to travel, deprived him of liberty without due process in violation of the Fifth Amendment, and implicated the Equal Protection clause of the Fourteenth Amendment. In July 1998, the district court, in *Mason v. Tucson* (D. Arizona, 1998) granted a temporary injunction against enforcing the law, saying the zone restrictions were overbroad. Subsequently, the parties entered into settlement negotiations.

CHAPTER 7
THE HEALTH OF THE HOMELESS

LIVING IN PUBLIC: INCREASED HEALTH PROBLEMS

Virtually all Americans suffer illness and disease at some time in their lives, but for people experiencing homelessness and poverty, illness all too often means serious health concerns or premature death. Health problems that may not be so apparent at other income levels, like alcoholism, mental illnesses, diabetes, and depression, become visible and more pronounced with homeless people. Other, more serious illnesses are almost exclusively associated with poverty. Homeless people suffer from more types of illnesses, for longer periods of time, and with more harmful consequences than housed people.

The Homeless/Morbidity Connection

Researcher Mary Ann Burg, in "Health Problems of Sheltered Homeless Women and their Dependent Children" (*Health and Social Work*, 1994), explored the relationship between ill health and poverty and categorized the health problems of homeless women and their dependent children living in shelters. Burg's study revealed three general classifications of illnesses related to homelessness:

- Illnesses resulting from homelessness

- Illnesses intensified by the limited health care access of the homeless

- Illnesses associated with the psychosocial burdens of homelessness

Poor health is not only a result of homelessness, but has been reported as a cause of homelessness. Thirteen percent of homeless patients surveyed in a national study published in 1987 (Wright and Weber, *Health Care for the Homeless Information Resource Center*, Policy Research Associates, Delmar, New York) stated that poor physical health was a factor in their becoming homeless. Of those patients, half said health was a "major factor," and 15 percent stated that it was the "single most important" factor.

The Homeless/Mortality Connection

Doctor J. D. O'Connell, a physician with Boston's Health Care for the Homeless (HCH) program, noted a rate of death among homeless patients that appeared to be higher than that of the general population. He initiated a research study ("Death on the Streets," *Harvard Medical Alumni Bulletin*, Winter 1997) to attempt to uncover any causal links (common traits) between homelessness and higher mortality. O'Connell concluded that while the causes of the higher morbidity and mortality rates among Boston's homeless people are complex, there are elements of the homeless life that encourage early death. Some of these are: exposure to extremes of weather and temperature; crowded shelter living, which increases the spread of communicable diseases such as tuberculosis and pneumonia; violence; the high frequency of medical and psychiatric illnesses; substance abuse; and inadequate nutrition.

A 1998 study of 558 homeless adults in Boston, Massachusetts, conducted by the Inner City Health Program (*Risk Factors for Death in Homeless Adults in Boston*), found that males, whites, and substance abusers were most likely to die while living on the streets. The strongest risk factors for death were AIDS, renal (kidney) disease, recurrent cold-related injuries, liver disease, and arrhythmia (irregular heartbeat). A history of substance abuse involving alcohol or injected drugs also increased the risk of mortality.

The Causes

Health care experts agree that the prevalence of illness and early death are greater in the poor and homeless population due to the following socioeconomic conditions:

- Poor diet

- Inadequate sleeping locations

- Contagion from overcrowded shelters

FIGURE 7.1

Growth in the number of uninsured Americans, 1994–1999

SOURCE: "Figure 1: Growth in the Number of Uninsured Americans, 1994–1999," in *Health Insurance Characteristics and Trends in the Uninsured Population,* General Accounting Office, Washington DC, March 13, 2001

- Limited facilities for daily hygiene
- Exposure to the elements
- Exposure to violence
- Social isolation
- Lack of health insurance

The Severity of the Problem

There is a growing belief in the health care field that homelessness needs to be considered in epidemic terms—that massive increases in homelessness may result in a hastened spread of illness and disease, overwhelming the health care system. Researcher W. R. Breakey recognizes the morbidity rates among the homeless as a major public health concern. In a 1997 article in the *American Journal of Public Health* ("It's Time for the Public Health Community to Declare War on Homelessness"), Breakey proposes that homelessness be responded to with the same urgency as an epidemic of an infectious disease. He urges public health officials to address larger issues—socioeconomic elements such as housing availability and wages—in order to truly cure afflicted individuals.

In the last decade, the scope of health issues regarding the impoverished and homeless in the United States has grown as a result of increases in the number of uninsured Americans. As reported in a study by the GAO (General Accounting Office) in 1999, 42.1 million people in the United States lacked health insurance. (See Figure 7.1.) More than one-third of persons living in poverty had no health insurance of any kind. A recent analysis of Health Care for the Homeless (HCH) projects (J. O'Connell, et al., *Life and Death on the Streets: Health Care Reform*

FIGURE 7.2

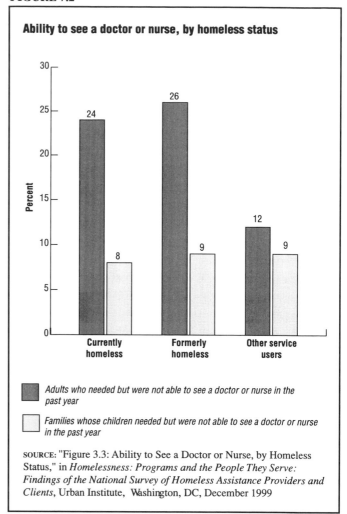

Ability to see a doctor or nurse, by homeless status

SOURCE: "Figure 3.3: Ability to See a Doctor or Nurse, by Homeless Status," in *Homelessness: Programs and the People They Serve: Findings of the National Survey of Homeless Assistance Providers and Clients,* Urban Institute, Washington, DC, December 1999

and Homelessness, National Health Care for the Homeless Council, 1997) found that the number of uninsured persons seeking treatment is increasing overall, and the coverage held by many others would not carry them through a catastrophic illness.

The Health Costs of Street Living

The rates of both chronic and acute health problems are extremely high among the homeless population. With the exception of obesity, strokes, and cancer, homeless people are far more likely than the nonhomeless to suffer from every category of chronic health problem. Conditions that require regular, uninterrupted treatment, such as tuberculosis (TB), HIV/AIDS, diabetes, hypertension, malnutrition, severe dental problems, addictive disorders, and mental disorders, are extremely difficult to treat or control among those without adequate housing.

Street living comes with a set of health conditions that living in a home does not. Human beings without shelter tend to fall prey to parasites, frostbite, leg ulcers, and infections. Homeless people are also at greater risk of physical and psychological trauma resulting from muggings, beatings, and rape. With no safe place to store belongings, proper storage or administration of medications becomes difficult. In addition, some homeless people with mental disorders may use drugs or alcohol to self-medicate, and those with addictive disorders are more susceptible to HIV and other communicable diseases.

Homeless people may also lack the ability to access some of the fundamental rituals of self-care: bed rest, good nutrition, and good personal hygiene. The luxury of "taking it easy for a day or two," for example, is almost impossible for homeless people; they must often keep walking or remain standing all day in order to avoid criminal charges. (See Table 6.1.)

Unwell homeless people also remain untreated longer than their sheltered counterparts because obtaining food and shelter takes priority over health care. As a result, relatively minor illnesses go untreated until they develop into major emergencies, requiring expensive acute care treatment and long-term recovery.

The Urban Institute studied the clients of homeless health care centers across the United States and reported that in the previous year, 25 percent of the clients studied had needed medical attention but were not able to see a doctor or a nurse. The same study also revealed that recently homeless people were even less likely to receive medical help when needed (26 percent). (See Figure 7.2.)

The increase in health neglect among the newly housed is most likely due to: 1) the loss of convenient health care in centers or shelters, 2) the habit of enduring untreated ailments, and/or 3) a lack of health care benefits (common among people below the poverty level). A 1999 study by the General Accounting Office revealed that 37 percent of those people below the official poverty level ($17,029 annual income for a family of four) were likely to be uninsured. (See Figure 7.3.) Of those people earning four times the poverty level (about $68,000) or more, only 8 percent were uninsured.

The results of a study published in February 2000 (L. Gelberg, et al., "The Behavioral Model for Vulnerable Populations: Application to Medical Care Use and Outcomes for Homeless People," *Health Services Research*) on the prevalence of certain conditions of disease among homeless adults found that 37 percent suffered from functional vision impairment, 36 percent from skin/leg/foot problems, and 31 percent tested positive for tuberculosis (TB). The authors of the study indicated that better health increased among homeless people having a community clinic or private physician as a regular source of care. The research study also concluded that successful clinical treatment of the homeless is best accomplished if accompanied by efforts to find them permanent housing.

FIGURE 7.3

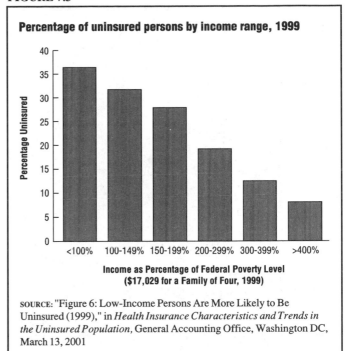

Percentage of uninsured persons by income range, 1999

Income as Percentage of Federal Poverty Level
($17,029 for a Family of Four, 1999)

SOURCE: "Figure 6: Low-Income Persons Are More Likely to Be Uninsured (1999)," in *Health Insurance Characteristics and Trends in the Uninsured Population*, General Accounting Office, Washington DC, March 13, 2001

PHYSICAL AILMENTS OF HOMELESS PEOPLE

According to a March 2000 survey of the homeless performed by The Institute of Outcomes Research for the Hartford Community Health Partnership (E. B. O'Keefe, R. Maljanian, and M. McCormack, *Hartford Homeless Health Survey*), 87 percent of survey respondents reported a prior diagnosis of at least one of seventeen chronic conditions. The most prevalent of these chronic conditions were drug and alcohol abuse, depression and other mental illnesses, hypertension, chronic bronchitis and emphysema, HIV/AIDS, asthma, and arthritis. Comparing the responses from the homeless survey against the rates for the general Hartford, Connecticut, population revealed that depression was almost twice as likely among the homeless (41 percent) than among the general population (23 percent) and the rate of chronic bronchitis and emphysema among homeless survey respondents was 22.7 percent, three times that of Hartford's general population. While these chronic diseases exist throughout the general population, difficulty in providing treatment to the homeless makes them worse, as do hunger and malnutrition.

Tuberculosis

Several kinds of acute, nonspecific respiratory diseases are common among homeless people. These diseases are spread by living in groups and overcrowded shelters, in stressful situations, and without adequate nutrition. Tuberculosis (TB), a disease at one time almost eliminated from the general American population, has become a major health problem among the homeless. This disease is associated with exposure, poor diet, alcoholism,

TABLE 7.1

Tuberculosis cases by homeless status, 1999

Reporting area	Total cases	Cases with information on homeless status		Percent of cases in homeless persons[1]
		No.	%	
United States	**17,531**	**16,808**	**95.9**	**6.3**
Alabama	314	312	99.4	3.8
Alaska	61	61	100.0	3.3
Arizona	262	258	98.5	14.0
Arkansas	181	180	75.0	3.9
California	3,606	3,554	98.6	6.6
Colorado	88	88	100.0	12.5
Connecticut	121	119	98.3	9.2
Delaware	34	34	100.0	2.9
District of Columbia	70	70	100.0	14.3
Florida	1,277	1,276	99.9	8.7
Georgia	665	632	95.0	7.0
Hawaii	184	184	100.0	0.0
Idaho	16	15	93.8	6.7
Illinois	825	796	96.5	6.7
Indiana	150	133	88.7	3.0
Iowa	58	48	82.8	6.3
Kansas	69	64	92.8	1.6
Kentucky	209	205	98.1	12.2
Louisiana	357	350	98.0	5.7
Maine	23	23	100.0	8.7
Maryland	294	293	99.7	3.1
Massachusetts	270	269	99.6	4.5
Michigan	351	342	97.4	3.5
Minnesota	201	201	100.0	3.0
Mississippi	215	215	100.0	1.4
Missouri	208	197	94.7	14.2
Montana	14	14	100.0	35.7
Nebraska	18	18	100.0	11.1
Nevada	93	92	98.9	8.7
New Hampshire	19	18	94.7	0.0
New Jersey	571	571	100.0	5.3
New Mexico	64	64	100.0	7.8
New York State[2]	377	372	98.7	1.9
New York City	1,460	987	67.6	—
North Carolina	488	486	99.6	7.0
North Dakota	7	6	85.7	16.7
Ohio	317	313	98.7	7.3
Oklahoma	208	208	100.0	11.1
Oregon	123	121	98.4	10.7
Pennsylvania	454	423	93.2	2.1
Rhode Island	53	52	98.1	0.0
South Carolina	315	314	99.7	3.8
South Dakota	21	21	100.0	14.3
Tennessee	382	376	98.4	7.4
Texas	1,649	1,649	100.0	6.6
Utah	40	40	100.0	17.5
Vermont	3	3	100.0	0.0
Virginia	334	334	100.0	2.7
Washington	258	257	99.6	6.2
West Virginia	41	37	90.2	13.5
Wisconsin	110	110	100.0	4.5
Wyoming	3	3	100.0	0.0
American Samoa[3]	4	4	100.0	0.0
Fed. States of Micronesia[3]	...	...	...	...
Guam[3]	69	69	100.0	0.0
N. Mariana Islands[3]	66	66	100.0	0.0
Puerto Rico[3]	200	200	100.0	3.0
Republic of Palau[3]	11	11	100.0	0.0
U.S. Virgin Islands[3]	...	...	...	...

[1]Homeless within past 12 months. Percentage for U.S. based on 52 reporting areas (50 states, New York City, and the District of Columbia). Percentages shown only for reporting areas with information reported for ≥75% of cases.
[2]Excludes New York City.
[3]Not included in U.S. totals.
Ellipses indicate data not available.

SOURCE: "Table 24. Tuberculosis Cases by Homeless Status: 59 Reporting Areas, 1999," Centers for Disease Control & Prevention, National Center for HIV, STD, and TB Prevention, Atlanta, GA, 1999.

and other illnesses that lower the body's resistance to infection. TB is spread by personal contact, making it a potential hazard not only to shelter residents, but also to the general public.

From 1953 to 1988, the United States experienced a decrease of 5 percent per year in the number of reported TB cases. However, in 1988 the number of TB cases began to rise. Increased shelter use and other unsanitary, crowded living situations among the homeless are responsible for the spread of the disease. Poor ventilating systems and the inability to quarantine victims have allowed it to become prevalent. In 1999 the Centers for Disease Control reported that 6.3 percent of the homeless population in the United States had TB. State-by-state breakdowns give some indication of the contagious nature of tuberculosis. (See Table 7.1.) In 1999, for example, Montana reported that 35.7 percent of its homeless population tested positive for the disease, while states like Wyoming, Vermont, and Hawaii had no cases of TB among the homeless.

Clinical data from National Health Care for the Homeless finds prevalence rates for tuberculosis to be 100 to 300 times higher among the homeless than among the overall population. Furthermore, substance abuse and the prevalence of other diseases, such as HIV, make homeless people less able to resist infection. An additional contributing factor has been the emergence of drug-resistant strains of TB. Experts report that to control the spread of TB, the homeless must receive frequent screenings for TB, and the infected must get long-term care and rest.

Malnutrition

Homeless people face a daily challenge to fulfill their basic need for food. Not only are they often hungry, but undernourishment and vitamin deficiency can also cause or aggravate other physical signs and symptoms. The U.S. Public Health Service estimates that 20 to 44 percent of the homeless are malnourished (lacking in vitamins and minerals), and 32 percent are underweight. More than one-third of homeless adults go without eating at least one day a week, and when they do eat, they eat only half the daily amount of food recommended by the U.S. Department of Agriculture (USDA). A 1999 study by the Association of Gospel Rescue Missions revealed that 45.6 percent of people living below 200 percent of the poverty level had difficulties or worries about affording food, compared to only half that figure (23.2 percent) among the general population. (See Table 7.2.)

Furthermore, the diet of the homeless is generally not balanced or of good quality, even among those who live in shelters or cheap motels. The low quality and quantity of meals is likely due to the inability of the homeless to afford high-quality food and their lack of access to food storage and cooking facilities. Consequently, homeless people often rely on ready-cooked meals, fast-food restaurants,

TABLE 7.2

Affordability of food and housing, by race and ethnicity, 1997–1999

Nonelderly Americans living in families that worried about or experienced difficulties affording food

Below 200 percent of poverty level	1997	1999
White, non-Hispanic	43.3	38.4v
Hispanic, all races	56.1	53.9
Black, non-Hispanic	57.0	56.3
All races/ethnicities	49.0	45.6v
Above 200 percent of poverty level		
White, non-Hispanic	11.9	10.5v
Hispanic, all races	22.9	23.7
Black, non-Hispanic	22.3	23.9
All races/ethnicities	13.9	13.1
All incomes		
White, non-Hispanic	19.9	17.1v
Hispanic, all races	43.0	40.6
Black, non-Hispanic	39.4	40.1
All races/ethnicities	25.6	23.2v

Nonelderly Americans living in families with problems paying their mortgage, rent or utility bills

Below 200 percent poverty level		
White, non-Hispanic	24.2	23.2
Hispanic, all races	24.5	24.9
Black, non-Hispanic	29.8	33.1
All races/ethnicities	25.4	25.5
Above 200 percent poverty level		
White, non-Hispanic	6.5	6.2
Hispanic, all races	11.6	12.3
Black, non-Hispanic	13.2	16.1
All races/ethnicities	7.4	7.6
All incomes		
White, non-Hispanic	11.1	10.2v
Hispanic, all races	19.4	19.4
Black, non-Hispanic	21.4	24.6^
All races/ethnicities	13.4	13.2

Note: "All races/ethnicities" includes Native Americans and Asian Americans. These indicators measure concerns about food and housing affordability during the last 12 months. Figures in boldface represent values that are statistically significantly different from the 1999 national average at the 0.10 confidence level. The symbols "^" and "v" represent statistically significant increases and decreases, respectively, between 1997 and 1999 at the 0.10 confidence level.

SOURCE: "Affordability of Food and Housing, by Race and Ethnicity, 1997–1999," in *1999 Snapshots of America's Families II: Key Findings by Race and Ethnicity*, Urban Institute, Washington, DC, 2000.

garbage cans, and the sometimes infrequent meal schedules of free food sources, such as shelters, soup kitchens, and drop-in centers. Nearly two-thirds of soup kitchens serve only one meal a day, and many shelters that serve meals— and not all of them do—serve only two meals a day. The U.S. Conference of Mayors reported in 2000 that 13 percent of the 25 cities surveyed said that the food provided in emergency shelters was not enough to meet the needs of the homeless and poor. (See Table 2.2.) About half (46 percent) of the cities reported turning people away in the previous year, and 71 percent expected the demand for emergency food to increase in the coming year.

In addition, alcoholism, drug use, mental illness (especially severe depression), and physical illness contribute to nutritional deficiencies or lack of appetite. Some soup kitchens and shelters exclude persons high on drugs from partaking of meals at their facilities. Persons on drugs may not be interested in food when they are high, and they can lose many pounds. Some advocates for the homeless suggest providing vitamin and mineral supplements to homeless drug users.

Skin and Blood Vessel Disorders

Frequent exposure to severe weather, insect bites, and other infestations make skin lesions fairly common among the homeless. Being forced to sit or stand for extended periods results in many homeless people being plagued with edema (swelling of the feet and legs), varicose veins, and skin ulcerations. This population is more prone to conditions that can lead to chronic phlebitis (inflammation of the veins). A homeless person with circulatory problems who sleeps sitting up in a doorway or a bus station can develop open lacerations that may become infected or maggot-infested if left untreated.

Regular baths and showers are luxuries to most homeless people, so many suffer from various forms of dermatitis (inflammation of the skin), often due to infestations of lice or scabies (a contagious skin disease caused by a parasitic mite that burrows under the skin to deposit eggs, causing intense itching). The lack of bathing increases the opportunity for infection to develop in cuts and other lacerations.

AIDS

The lack of affordable and appropriate housing can be an acute crisis for persons living with HIV/AIDS. Persons with HIV/AIDS not only need a safe shelter that provides protection and comfort, but also a base from which to receive services, care, and support.

The University of California at San Francisco, in *HIV Prevention: Looking Back, Looking Ahead* (1995), reported that almost half the homeless are estimated to have two or more of the risk factors associated with HIV—unprotected sex with multiple partners, injection drug use (IDU), sex with an IDU partner, or the exchange of unprotected sex for money or drugs. One-fourth report three or more risk factors. Having multiple sex partners is a risk for HIV, but it is extremely difficult for homeless people to form safe or stable intimate relationships due to drug use, mental illness, violence, or transient living conditions. Most homeless women experience rape or battery, and many women and children engage in "survival sex," or the exchange of sex for money, drugs, food, or housing.

THE MENTAL HEALTH OF HOMELESS PEOPLE

In a 1998 study of 132 homeless adults (E. M. Reichenbach, et al., "The Community Health Nursing Implications of the Self-Reported Health Status of a Local Homeless Population," *Public Health Nurse*, December 1998), researchers explored the personal characteristics and the health and health-related concerns of homeless health clinic clients. The study examined the significant differences in health and well-being between homeless shelter residents and nonshelter residents. The homeless population studied featured a majority of males, average age in the mid-thirties, a high rate of unemployment, and a low rate of health insurance. One-third of respondents reported their own health status as fair or poor. Joint problems and cardiovascular disease were the two most common physical ailments mentioned, while depression was the most common self-identified mental health problem. The most common fear mentioned by study participants was loneliness, but homeless people staying in shelters reported this fear much less often than those who did not stay in shelters.

Perceptions of and about Mental Illness and the Homeless

When mentally ill patients are released from institutions, they are often left on their own, with either inadequate or no community-based treatment centers and housing. These people are often suspicious of the mental health system, which may have either failed or abused them in the past. Many homeless people do not realize how ill they are and how dependent they are on regular treatment, while others no longer believe the system can or will help them.

There is also a danger of classifying homeless persons as mentally ill, when their "abnormal" actions may actually be behavior caused by social and economic problems. For example, many homeless women act strangely and neglect personal hygiene as a way to protect themselves from attack. A 1988 report on homeless women in San Francisco (C. J. Cooper, "Brutal Lives of Homeless S.F. Women," *San Francisco Examiner*, December 1988) revealed a high rate of rape and sexual assault—some of the women had been raped as many as 17 times. The report stated that to protect themselves from attack, homeless women would wear 10 pairs of panty hose at once and bundle up in layers of clothing.

Treatment and Prevalence

Mentally ill homeless people present special problems for health care workers. They may not be as cooperative and motivated as other patients. Because of their limited resources, they may have difficulty getting transportation to treatment centers. They frequently forget to show up for appointments or take medications. They are often unkempt because of the lack of facilities for personal hygiene. The addition of drug abuse can make them unruly or unresponsive. Among people with severe mental disorders, those at greatest risk of homelessness are both the most severely ill and the most difficult to help.

Although there is controversy about the rate of mental disorders among homeless populations, it is certainly greater among the homeless than the general population. The 2000 U.S. Conference of Mayors study reported that an average of 22 percent of the homeless in the 24 surveyed cities were considered severely mentally ill. (See Table 2.2.) This is a 3 percent increase over 1999 (19 percent), but the second lowest reported percentage since 1985.

SUBSTANCE ABUSE

The abuse of alcohol and other drugs has long been recognized as a major factor contributing to the problems of the homeless. Being intoxicated or high in public has long been considered socially unacceptable. Housed substance abusers have the luxury of staying out of public scrutiny when in such a condition. But homeless people have no place else to be except outside. Consequently, homeless substance abusers are often more visible than the general population, which may lead to inflated statistics. According to the National Coalition for the Homeless, though, in *No Open Door: Breaking the Lock on Addiction Recovery for Homeless People* (December 1998), the number of addictive disorders per capita within the homeless population is nearly twice that of the general population, and even higher in certain localities.

In "Substance Use Among Runaway and Homeless Youth in Three National Samples" (*American Journal of Public Health*, 1997), researchers Greene, Ennett, and Ringwalt found that 81 percent of street youth and 67 percent of homeless youth in shelters were using alcohol. In addition, 75 percent of street youth and 52 percent of sheltered youth were using marijuana, and 26 percent of street youth and 8 percent of sheltered youth were using crack cocaine. Among housed youth, 64 percent used alcohol, 25 percent used marijuana, and 2 percent used crack cocaine.

The U.S. Conference of Mayors found that in 2000, 37 percent of the homeless in surveyed cities were substance abusers, up 6 percent from the 1999 figure but down by 11 percent from the high of 48 percent in 1993. (See Table 2.2.)

Dual Diagnosis and Substance Abuse

The National Institute of Mental Health (NIMH) and the National Institute on Alcohol Abuse and Alcoholism (NIAAA) report that mental illness and substance abuse frequently occur together. Clinicians call this co-occurring disorders, or dual diagnosis. Experts report that in the absence of appropriate treatment, persons with mental illness often resort to "self-medication," using alcohol or drugs to silence the voices or calm the fears that torment them. Homeless people with dual diagnoses are frequently excluded from mental health programs because of treatment problems created by their substance abuse and are excluded from substance abuse programs due to problems in treating their mental illness. Experts report that the lack of an integrated system of care plays a major role in their

recurrent homelessness. They stress that transitional or assisted housing initiatives for homeless substance abusers must realistically address the issue of abstinence and design measures for handling relapses that do not place people back on the streets.

Substance Abusers at Greater Risk of Homelessness?

Some people fear that recent welfare policy changes may increase homelessness among impoverished people with addiction disorders. In 1996 Congress passed the Personal Responsibility and Work Opportunity Reconciliation Act (PL 104-193), which, among other things, denies Social Security Income (SSI) and Social Security Disability Insurance (SSDI) benefits and, by extension, Medicaid, to people whose addictions are a "contributing factor" in their disability.

SPECIAL POPULATION CONCERNS

Children

While a quarter of all homeless people may suffer from mental illness, and many more have a past or current drug or alcohol addiction, these common stereotypes of the homeless do not fit a significant segment of the homeless population. Children under 18 years of age, for example, make up almost 10 percent of the homeless.

One research team (E. R. Danseco and E. W. Holden, "Are There Different Types of Homeless Families? A Typology of Homeless Families Based on Cluster Analysis," *Family Relations*, 1998) sought to identify different types of homeless families and to examine children from these families. The researchers studied 180 families, with a total of 348 children, that participated in a comprehensive health care program for children of homeless families. The results showed that homeless children consistently exhibited greater behavior problems and showed a trend of poorer cognitive, academic, and adaptive behaviors than children in the general population.

Similar results were found in a 1999 Urban Institute study. Figure 7.4 shows that poor children are less involved in school than their more well-off peers—41 percent of children above 200 percent of the poverty level have a high engagement in school, versus 34 percent of children below 200 percent of the poverty level. Lower-income children had 4 percent more behavioral and emotional problems, skipped school 7 percent more often, were expelled or suspended more than twice as often, and reported fair or poor health more than three times as frequently as children above 200 percent of the poverty level.

Veterans

The U.S. Department of Veterans Affairs (VA) estimates that 250,000 veterans are homeless on any given night. Twice that number may be homeless in a given year. A one-day count in September 1997 revealed that

FIGURE 7.4

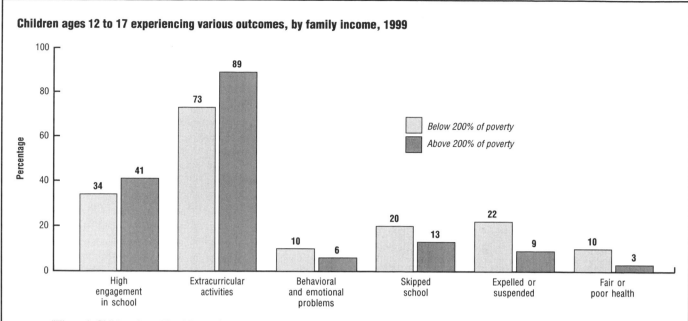

Children ages 12 to 17 experiencing various outcomes, by family income, 1999

SOURCE: "Figure 3: Children Ages 12 to 17 Experiencing Various Child Outcomes, by Family Income, 1999," in *1999 Snapshots of America's Families II: Children's Behavior and Well-Being*, Urban Institute, Washington, DC, 2000

approximately one-fourth of the patients in VA hospitals were homeless. In 2000 the U.S. Conference of Mayors reported that veterans made up 15 percent of the homeless in the surveyed cities, a decrease of 7 percent from two years ago.

To some, the homelessness of veterans is hard to understand. Since World War II, U.S. veterans have been offered a broad range of special benefits, including educational assistance, home loan guarantees, pension and disability payments, and free health care. In fact, veterans consistently have higher median incomes, lower rates of poverty and unemployment, and better education than U.S. males in similar age groups. Veterans, those observers claim, should be less vulnerable to homelessness than other Americans.

The belief that veterans become homeless because of combat-related stress is receiving more attention of late. Health care professionals believe that there may be a link between the persistence of post-traumatic stress disorder (PTSD) in veterans and the stresses of street living, though research on this topic is as yet inconclusive.

Victims of Violence

VIOLENCE TOWARD HOMELESS WOMEN. Angela Browne, Ph.D., and Shari Bassuk, in a study funded by the National Institute of Mental Health and the Maternal and Child Health Bureau, found that lifetime prevalence rates of physical and sexual assault among homeless women were particularly high. The study, "Intimate Violence in the Lives of Homeless and Poor Housed Women:

Prevalence and Patterns in an Ethnically Diverse Sample" (*American Journal of Orthopsychiatry*, April 1999), which surveyed both homeless and very poor housed women, found that although violence by intimate male partners was high in both groups, homeless women experienced violence at a somewhat higher rate (63.3 percent) than poor housed women (58 percent).

Homeless women (41 percent) were more likely than housed women (33 percent) to report a male partner threatening suicide. More than 36 percent of homeless women said their partner had threatened to kill them, compared to 31 percent of housed women. Almost 27 percent of homeless women and 19.5 percent of poor housed women needed or received medical treatment because of physical violence.

HATE CRIMES. According to the National Coalition for the Homeless (NCH), homeless advocates are demanding that crimes against the homeless be defined as hate crimes. Determining how many of these crimes occur is difficult. Some factors that have an effect on the accuracy of the count are:

• The bodies of the victims are not always discovered.

• Bodies may be badly decomposed, preventing accurate identification of the cause of death.

• Local authorities may rule causes of death other than violence.

• Survivors do not always report crimes, and murdered victims cannot tell their own stories.

In some instances, cases may appear to be accidents, rather than purposeful attacks. For example, in Rapid City, South Dakota, in less than two years, eight homeless men drowned in a local trout stream. At first the police called these accidental drownings, because the men all had high blood-alcohol levels. However, other homeless men insisted that the victims had been pushed into the stream as they lay passed out from alcohol. The insistence of the homeless population eventually convinced the Rapid City police to consider the drownings possible homicides.

The available numbers indicate a significant increase in hate crimes against the homeless. In 1999 the NCH counted 29 hate crime murders of homeless people; in 2000 they reported that 61 such crimes had occurred. Health Care for the Homeless reported 43 cases of hate crime murders and another 23 cases of nonfatal violence against the homeless in 2000. Victims were mainly male and ranged in age from 18 to 72.

In an Urban Institute analysis of 1996 data, 22 percent of the studied population reported being physically assaulted or beaten at some time while they were homeless. (See Figure 7.5.) In what's often called "bum-bashing" or "troll-busting," homeless people are attacked by gangs, usually made up of juveniles. The following list provides a few examples of such attacks:

- In 1999 in Denver, Colorado, two homeless people were beheaded and five others were attacked and killed by three people, all of whom were age 20 or younger at the time.

- In October 2000 in Honolulu, Hawaii, firefighters responded to a small rubbish fire and discovered the wheelchair of a 48-year-old disabled homeless man on fire. The man appeared to have been beaten and was lying unconscious five feet from the fire. He died before authorities could question him.

- In November 2000 two men kidnapped a homeless man, tied him up, and poured battery acid on his genitals while they threatened to kill him with the drop cord they had tied around his neck.

- In April 2001 a 50-year-old Las Vegas man, called "Rusty" by his friends, was bludgeoned to death early one morning by a group of three or four youths. Reportedly the perpetrators happened upon Rusty at a campsite and began kicking and beating him as he lay in his sleeping bag. The county coroner ruled the slaying a death by "massive blunt force trauma." The victim had told an acquaintance that he had been assaulted on three other occasions in the previous month. The first of those beatings sent him to the hospital, but the others went unreported.

Advocates worry that violence against the homeless will increase as the number of homeless people continues

FIGURE 7.5

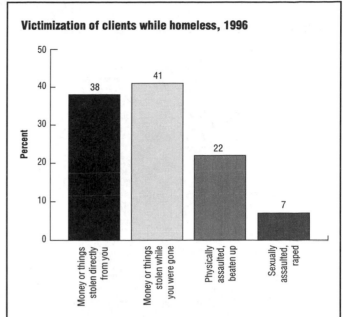

Victimization of clients while homeless, 1996

SOURCE: "Figure 2.10: Victimization of Clients while Homeless." *Homelessness: Programs and the People They Serve: Findings of the National Survey of Homeless Assistance Providers and Clients*, Urban Institute, Washington, DC, December 1999.

to rise. This type of violence adversely affects the abilities of homeless people to achieve a better life—the physical injuries sustained from burning or beating, for example, can leave a formerly healthy individual with a crippling disability, preventing him or her from working. Also, the terror of anticipating or surviving this type of violence can lead to severe and permanent psychological trauma.

The cost of attending to these types of critical injuries is huge. Skin grafts and multiple surgeries needed for the most grievous injuries are costly. Necessary recuperation time tends to be longer than for illnesses of a nonviolent nature, resulting in higher hospital, medicine, and after-care costs. Many of the victims, however, receive inadequate recuperation time, which leads to further health problems and additional costs in the long run.

PROBLEMS IN HEALING THE HOMELESS

According to Health Care for the Homeless (HCH), the growth of managed health care, with its limited options, the increasing homeless population, and the negative health aspects of welfare reform have made it impossible for homeless health care programs to reach the majority of homeless people in America. A 1997 study by the Bureau of Primary Health Care (J. O'Connell, et al., *Increased Demand and Decreased Capacity: Challenges to the McKinney Act's Health Care for the Homeless Program*, Health Care for the Homeless) found that homeless health care projects were experiencing significant growth in homelessness in their communities. At the same time,

FIGURE 7.6

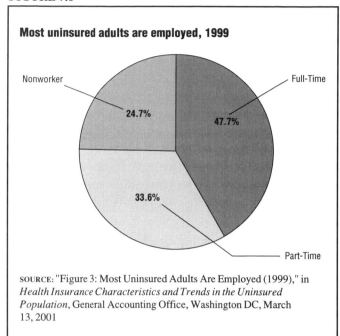

Most uninsured adults are employed, 1999

Nonworker 24.7%

Full-Time 47.7%

Part-Time 33.6%

SOURCE: "Figure 3: Most Uninsured Adults Are Employed (1999)," in *Health Insurance Characteristics and Trends in the Uninsured Population*, General Accounting Office, Washington DC, March 13, 2001

financial support for HCH programs was diminishing. As a result, HCH projects have been forced to reduce program staffing, waiting lists have lengthened, and turn-away rates have increased.

The Insurance Factor

There is a persistent misconception that people who do not have health insurance somehow get the care they need, especially when they have serious health problems. In fact, the uninsured have numerous problems that are not getting care. A national survey conducted by the Agency for Healthcare Research and Quality of the U.S. Department of Health and Human Services compared the health care received by insured and uninsured nonelderly people who have five common health conditions: heart disease, hypertension, high blood cholesterol, arthritis, and chronic back pain. The study demonstrates that the likelihood of being able to access medicine, doctors, or other treatment for these conditions differs greatly, depending on insurance status. Among the report's (*Getting Less Care: The Uninsured with Chronic Health Conditions*, Families USA Publication, 2001) findings are:

- Uninsured people with arthritis are more than five times as likely to receive no prescriptions of any kind as their insured counterparts.

- Among people diagnosed with high blood pressure, the uninsured are more than twice as likely to have had no blood pressure check in the past year.

- Uninsured people with heart disease have 28 percent fewer visits to physicians' offices, clinics, or hospital outpatient centers than insured people with heart disease.

- Among those with hypertension and arthritis, the uninsured are more than three and one-half times as likely as the insured to lack a usual source of care.

- For people with heart disease, one-quarter (26 percent) of the uninsured report that they or a family member did not receive care due to cost, compared to only 7 percent of the insured.

THE EFFECTS OF WELFARE REFORM ON HEALTH COVERAGE. Welfare reform has had an impact on health care for the homeless: Many families leaving welfare lose health insurance, despite continued Medicaid eligibility. A recent study found that 675,000 people, of whom 62 percent (400,000) were children, lost health insurance in 1997 as a result of federal welfare reform legislation (Families USA, 1999). Most of the children were probably still eligible for coverage under Medicaid. The number of people who lose health coverage due to welfare reform is certain to grow rather substantially in the years ahead.

Overall, in 15 states there was a decline in Medicaid health coverage every year from January 1996 through December 1999. The decline for the earlier two-year period January 1996 through January 1998 (16 percent) was slightly larger than the decline from January 1998 through December 1999 (13 percent).

A Families USA study of Medicaid and Children's Health Insurance Program (CHIP) enrollment in the 12 states with the most uninsured children found that from 1996 to 1999 nearly one million children lost Medicaid. But many of these children were then enrolled in newly expanded Medicaid programs or the new CHIP programs. While enrollment of children in Medicaid alone declined by 8.9 percent over these three years, combined Medicaid and CHIP enrollment dropped by only 2 percent.

THE WORKING UNINSURED POOR. Not only have former welfare recipients lost medical coverage, but low-income workers have as well. Nearly one million low-income parents in 15 states lost Medicaid coverage between 1996 and 2000, due largely to flaws in state implementation of welfare reform. While states have expanded eligibility levels so more children can qualify for coverage, few states have done so for parents. In July 2001 a report (*The Health Care Safety Net: Millions of Low-Income People Left Uninsured*) was released by the health care consumer group Families USA, showing that some 81 percent of low-income, uninsured adults (over 13 million people) did not qualify for Medicaid or other types of public health coverage in their state.

The GAO reports that most uninsured adults are employed. Figure 7.6 shows that in 1999 over three-fourths of those without health insurance were employed either full-time or part-time. The larger group of uninsured workers was the full-time employees, at 41.7

FIGURE 7.7

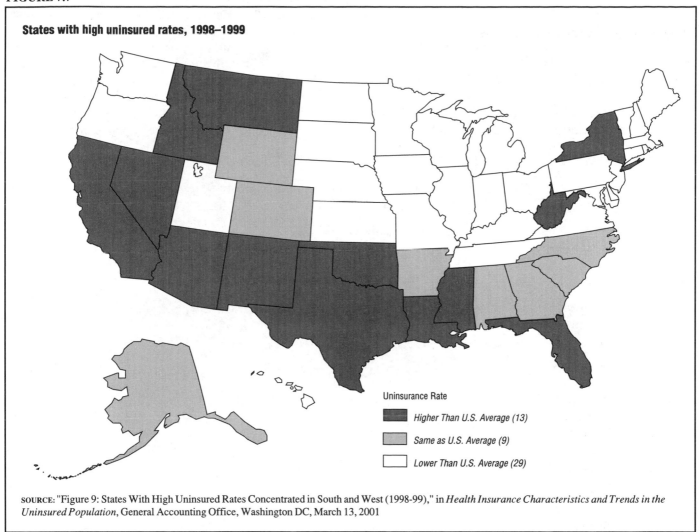

States with high uninsured rates, 1998–1999

Uninsurance Rate

■ Higher Than U.S. Average (13)

▨ Same as U.S. Average (9)

□ Lower Than U.S. Average (29)

SOURCE: "Figure 9: States With High Uninsured Rates Concentrated in South and West (1998-99)," in *Health Insurance Characteristics and Trends in the Uninsured Population*, General Accounting Office, Washington DC, March 13, 2001

percent, compared to part-time workers, who had a 33.6 percent uninsured rate.

Uninsured rates vary from state to state. Generally, the rate of uninsured adults is highest in the southern and western parts of the United States. Figure 7.7 illustrates the concentration of high uninsured rates in those geographic areas. Over half of the states have uninsured coverage rates lower than the national average. Only 13 out of the 50 states (16 percent) have higher than the national average. New Mexico has the highest rate at 26.6 percent, and Minnesota has the lowest rate at 9.6 percent.

HEALTH CARE FOR THE HOMELESS

In 1987 Congress passed the Stewart B. McKinney Homeless Assistance Act (PL 100-77) to provide services to the homeless, including job training, emergency shelter, education, and health care. Title VI of the Act funds Health Care for the Homeless (HCH) programs. HCH has become the national umbrella under which most homeless health care initiatives operate. In all, 123 HCH programs across the country provide health care to about a half mil-

lion people each year. In the year 2000 the government appropriated $88 million for HCH programs, up $8 million from 1999 and almost double the $46 million appropriation of 1987, the first year of the program.

The goal of the HCH program is to improve health status for homeless individuals and families by improving access to primary health care and substance abuse services. HCH provides outreach, counseling to clients explaining available services, case management, and linkages to services such as mental health treatment, housing, benefits, and other critical supports. Access to round-the-clock emergency services is available, and HCH also provides aid to the homeless in establishing eligibility for assistance and in obtaining services under entitlement programs.

HCH providers served nearly 430,000 men, women, and children during 2000. The majority of clients (62 percent) were male; 38 percent were female. Almost two-thirds of homeless clients were minorities: African Americans made up 42 percent; Hispanics, 16 percent; Asians/Pacific Islanders, 2 percent; and Native Americans/Alaskan natives, 2 percent.

Clients between the ages of 20 and 44 represented the largest portion of consumers served by the HCH programs (60 percent), followed by individuals between the ages of 45 and 64 (20 percent), children up to age 14 (13 percent), and teenagers between the ages of 15 and 19 (5 percent). Homeless persons over 65 comprised 2 percent of clients served.

Of clients seen in HCH centers, 45 percent lived in shelters at some point during treatment, while 12 percent lived on the street. The remainder lived in transitional housing, were doubled up with family or acquaintances, or were in some other type of living arrangement. The majority (70 percent) of HCH clients had no medical care resources. Of the remaining clients who had some type of insurance resource, 20 percent were Medicaid eligible (although not necessarily enrolled), 2 percent were Medicare eligible, 1 percent had private insurance, and 7 percent received some other type of public insurance.

IMPORTANT NAMES AND ADDRESSES

Association of Rescue Gospel Missions
1045 Swift St.
Kansas City, MO 64116-4127
(816) 471-8020
FAX: (816) 471-3718
URL: www.iugm.org

Center on Budget and Policy Priorities
820 1st St. NE, #510
Washington, DC 20002
(202) 408-1080
FAX: (202) 408-1056
E-mail: center@center.cbpp.org
URL: www.cbpp.org

Children's Defense Fund
25 E. St. NW
Washington, DC 20001
(202) 628-8787
FAX: (202) 662-3510
E-mail: cdfinfo@childrensdefense.org
URL: www.childrensdefense.org

Fannie Mae Foundation
4000 Wisconsin Ave. NW
North Tower, Suite One
Washington, DC 20016
(202) 274-8000
FAX: (202) 274-8132
URL: www.fanniemaefoundation.org

Food Research and Action Center
1875 Connecticut Ave. NW, #540
Washington, DC 20009-5728
(202) 986-2200
FAX: (202) 986-2525
URL: www.frac.org

Habitat for Humanity International
121 Habitat St.
Americus, GA 31709
(912) 924-6935
FAX: (912) 924-6541
E-mail: info@habitat.org
URL: www.habitat.org

Health Care for the Homeless Information Resource Center
Policy Research Associates, Inc.
262 Delaware Ave.
Delmar, NY 12054
FAX: (518) 439-7612
(888) 439-3300
E-mail: hch@prainc.com
URL: www.prainc.com/hch

Homes for the Homeless
36 Cooper Square, 6th Floor
New York, NY 10003
(212) 529-5252
FAX: (212) 529-7698
E-mail: hn4061@handset.org
URL: www.HomesfortheHomeless.com

Housing Assistance Council, Inc.
1025 Vermont Avenue, NW #606
Washington, DC 20005-3581
(202) 842-8600
FAX: (202) 347-3441
E-mail: hac@ruralhome.org
URL: www.ruralhome.org

Institute for Children and Poverty
36 Cooper Square, 6th Floor
New York, NY 10003
(212) 529-5252
FAX: (212) 529-7698
E-mail: hn4061@handsnet.org
URL: www.HomesfortheHomeless.com

Institute for Research on Poverty
University of Wisconsin-Madison
1180 Observatory Dr.
3412 Social Science Building
Madison, WI 53706
(608) 262-6358
FAX: (608) 265-3119
URL: www.ssc.wisc.edu/irp/

Interagency Council on the Homeless
451 Seventh St. SW, Ste. 7274

Washington, DC 20410
(202) 708-1480
FAX: (202) 708-3672
URL: www.hhs.gov/progsys/homeless/ich.htm

National Alliance of HUD Tenants
353 Columbus Avenue
Boston, MA 02116-6005
(617) 267-9564
FAX: (617) 267-4769
E-mail: webmaster@nycha-spotlight.com
URL: www.tenantsunion.org

National Alliance to End Homelessness
1518 K St. NW, #206
Washington, DC 20005
(202) 638-1526
FAX: (202) 638-4664
E-mail: naeh@naeh.org
URL: www.endhomelessness.org

National Center for Homeless Education
1100 West Market Street, Ste. 300
Greensboro, NC 27403
(336) 334-3211
FAX: (336) 574-3890
(800) 308-2145
E-mail: homeless@serve.org
URL: www.serve.org/nche

National Coalition for Homeless Veterans
333 1/2 Pennsylvania Ave., SE
Washington, DC 20003-1148
(202) 546-1969
FAX: (202) 546-2063
E-mail: nchv@nchv.org
URL: www.nchv.org

National Coalition for the Homeless
1612 K Street NW, Suite 1004
Washington, DC 20006-2802
(202) 737-6444
FAX: (202) 775-1316
E-mail: nch@ari.net
URL: www.nch.ari.net

National Health Care for the Homeless Council
P.O. Box 60427
Nashville, TN 37206-0427
(615) 226-2292
FAX: (615) 226-1656
E-mail: council@nhchc.org
URL: www.nhchc.org

National Housing Conference
815 Fifteenth Street, NW, Ste. 538
Washington, DC 20005-2201
(202) 393-5772, ext. 24
FAX: (202) 393-5656
E-mail: nhc@nhc.org
URL: www.nhc.org

National Housing Law Project
614 Grand Avenue, Ste. 320
Oakland, CA 94610
(510) 251-9400
FAX: (510) 251-0600
E-mail: HN0108@handsnet.org
URL: www.nhlp.org

National Law Center on Homelessness and Poverty
918 F Street NW, Suite 412
Washington, DC 20004
(202) 638-2535
FAX: (202) 628-2737
E-mail: nlchp@nlchp.org
URL: www.nlchp.org

National Low Income Housing Coalition
1012 14th St. NW, #610
Washington, DC 20005
(202) 662-1530
FAX: (202) 683-8639
E-mail: info@nlihc.org
URL: www.nlihc.org

National Resource Center on Homelessness and Mental Illness
Policy Research Associates
262 Delaware Avenue
Delmar, NY 12054
FAX: (518) 439-7612
(800) 444-7415
E-mail: nrc@prainc.com
URL: www.prainc.com/nrc

National Rural Housing Coalition
601 Pennsylvania Avenue, NW #850
Washington, DC 20004-2612
(202) 393-5229
FAX: (202) 393-3034
E-mail: NRHC@Rapoza.org
URL: www.rapoza.org/NRHC

National Student Campaign Against Hunger and Homelessness (NSCAHH)
11965 Venice Blvd., #408
Los Angeles, CA 90066
(310) 397-5270
FAX: (310) 391-0053
URL: www.pirg.org/nscahh

Second Harvest
116 S. Michigan Ave., Ste. 4
Chicago, IL 60603
(312) 263-2303
FAX: (312) 263-5626
URL: www.secondharvest.org

Urban Institute
2100 M St. NW
Washington, DC 20037
(202) 857-8702
FAX: (202) 223-3043
URL: www.urban.org

U.S. Conference of Mayors
Task Force on Hunger and Homelessness
1620 Eye St. NW, #400
Washington, DC 20006
(202) 293-7330
FAX: (202) 293-2352
URL: www.usmayors.org/uscm

U.S. Department of Education
Education for Homeless Children
600 Independence Ave. SW
Washington, DC 20202-6132
(202) 260-0997
URL: www.ed.gov

U.S. Department of Housing and Urban Development
HUD Building 451 7th St. SW
Washington, DC 20410
(202) 708-2690
FAX: (202) 708-3336
URL: www.hud.gov

U.S. Department of Veterans Affairs
Policy and Planning
810 Vermont Ave. NW
Washington, DC 20420
(202) 273-5033
FAX: (202) 273-9030
URL: www.va.gov

U.S. General Accounting Office
P.O. Box 6015
Gaithersburg, MD 20884-6015
(202) 512-6000
FAX: (301) 258-4066
URL: www.gao.gov

RESOURCES

Many different organizations study the homeless and the poor. Notable among them for their many large studies on homelessness is The Urban Institute. This organization's ongoing studies of the homeless are among the largest and most comprehensive in the United States. Their publications were a major source of information for this volume, especially: *America's Homeless II: Populations and Services* (2000); *Homelessness: Programs and the People They Serve. National Survey of Homeless Assistance Providers and Clients.* (December 1999), and; *On the Bottom Rung, A Profile of Americans in Low-Income Working Families* (October 2000). The Gale Group is very thankful for the use of their statistics.

Two other excellent sources of information on the national homeless population are the National League of Cities and the Association of Gospel Rescue Missions. The publication *The State of America's Cities: Seventeenth Annual Opinion Survey of Municipal Elected Officials* (National League of Cities, 2001), contains much valuable data on the scope of urban homelessness and how cities and regions try to deal with it. The *1999 Snap Shot Survey of the Homeless* (Association of Gospel Rescue Missions, November, 1999) also provides a great deal of information on the homeless population.

The many organizations that advocate for the homeless and their issues are also crucial sources for this book. The National Coalition for the Homeless is certainly one of the most important of these organizations. Their publication *Homelessness in America: Unabated and Increasing—A Ten-Year Perspective* (1997) is particularly recommended. The National Low Income Housing Coalition is another advocacy organization with much useful information on

homelessness, including *Out of Reach, The Growing Gap Between Housing Costs and Income of Poor People in the United States* (September 2000). The Gale Group is also grateful to the Economic Policy Institute, Health Care for the Homeless, National Coalition for Homeless Veterans, and the National Law Center on Homelessness & Poverty organizations for their coverage of important aspects of the homelessness issue.

No list of major sources of information on the homeless and poor would be complete without mentioning the federal government. While the government has done relatively few studies on the homeless itself since the 1980s, it remains the premier source of facts on many issues closely related to homelessness, including poverty, employment, welfare, and housing. There are far too many worthwhile publications to list here, but some particularly excellent sources of information that the Gale Group relied on in producing this book are: *Employment and Earnings,* (Bureau of Labor Statistics, January 2001); *Homelessness: Coordination and Evaluation of Programs Are Essential,* (General Accounting Office, 1999); *A Profile of the Working Poor, 1999,* (Bureau of Labor Statistics, February 2001); *Rental Housing Assistance—The Worsening Crisis,* (Office of Policy Development and Research, U.S. Department of Housing and Urban Development, March 2000); *Rural Homelessness: Focusing on the Needs of the Rural Homeless,* (Department of Agriculture, 1996). In addition to these specific publications, the Gale Group recommends that anyone interested in homelessness and related issues make use of the latest reports from the Bureau of the Census, the Department of Health and Human Services, and the Department of Housing and Urban Development.

INDEX

F

Families
  characteristics, 17
  children's living arrangements, 50–51
  homeless children and family
    characteristics, 20–21
  personal characteristics of family head,
    34*t*
  poverty rates by family type and presence
    of workers, 33(*f*3.5)
  single mothers, 32
Farm house, abandoned, *2*
Farmers Home Administration, 54
Federal government programs
  Affordable Housing Program, 62
  changing policies, 3
  Community Development Block Grants,
    61
  Community Investment Program, 62
  Consolidated Plan, 61
  Continuum of Care, 55
  Education for Homeless Children and
    Youth, 62
  Emergency Shelter Grants, 55, 56*t*
  expenditures for housing, 61*f*
  expenditures on children, 32*f*
  Federal Home Loan Bank programs, 62
  HIV/AIDS, housing for people with, 61
  HOME program, 61
  HOPE VI Program, 57–60
  Low Income Housing Tax Credit, 62
  need for more attention to affordable
    housing, 45–46
  New Deal, 2–3
  Projects for Transition from
    Homelessness (PATH), 62
  public housing projects, 56–60
  Runaway and Homeless Youth Program,
    62
  Rural Housing Programs, 62
  Section 8 vouchers, 58–60
  Shelter Plus Care program, 55, 56*t*
  Single Room Occupancy programs, 55,
    56*t*
  subsidized housing, 55–60
  Supportive Housing (Development)
    program, 55, 56*t*
  Tenant-Based Assistance, 58–60
  timeline of legislation and programs,
    53–54
  See also Assistance programs
Federal Home Loan Bank, 62
Food affordability, 73*t*
Food programs
  numbers of, 9*f*
  size of, 10(*f*1.4)
  for special populations, 11*f*
For-profit organizations, 10(*f*1.5)
Foscarinis, Maria, 66–67
Freedom of speech, 68
Funding
  cities and homeless counts, 7–8
  correlation between poverty rate and,
    31–32
  federal expenditures for housing, 61*f*
  federal expenditures on children, 32*f*

G

Gang attacks on homeless people, 77
GAO. *See* General Accounting Office (GAO)
Gender
  of homeless parents and living
    arrangements for children, 51
  homelessness by, 6*t*
  makeup of homeless population, 15–16
  median income by, 27*t*
  working poor, 35
  See also Women
General Accounting Office (GAO), 57
Gore, Edison, 7
Great Depression, 1–2, 53
Growing numbers of homeless, 13

H

Hate crimes, 76–77
Health issues, 69–80
  access to health care, by homeless status,
    70(*f*7.2), 71
  ailments, 71–74
  children, 75
  health care programs, 9*f*, 10(*f*1.4), 11*f*,
    77, 79–80
  HIV/AIDS, 74
  insurance, 70, 72, 78–79
  malnutrition, 73–74
  mental health, 74–75
  risk factors for death, 69
  skin and blood vessel disorders, 74
  veterans, 75–76
  victimization, 76–77
Historical attitudes, 1–3
HIV/AIDS, 61, 74
HOME Program, 61
Homeownership programs, 62
Homes for the Homeless, 9–10
"Hoovervilles," *3*
HOPE VI Program, 57–60
Housing
  affordability, 15, 17*f*, 45–46, 59*t*, 62, 73*t*
  federal expenditures for, 61*f*
  low-income, 42(*f*3.11), 45–46, 47, 60, 62
  privately owned, publicly assisted rental,
    60–61
  programs, 9*f*, 10(*f*1.4), 11*f*
  publicly assisted, 60–61
  reasons for lack of low-income, 47
  timeline of government legislation and
    programs, 53–54
  worst-case housing needs, 46, 47*f*
  See also Federal government programs
Housing Act of 1949, 54
Housing and Community Development Act
  of 1974, 54
Housing and Community Development
  Amendments, 54
Housing and Urban Development Act, 54
Housing and Urban-Rural Recovery Act of
  1983, 54
HUD. *See* Federal government programs
HUD Reform Act of 1989, 54
Hunger and homelessness, 14*t*

I

Incentives for low-income housing
  development, 47, 60, 62
Income levels, 40*t*
Institutionalized assistance, 42
Insurance, 70, 72, 78–79

J

Joint Free Library of Morristown, 67

K

Kennedy, John F., 54
Kreimer v. Bureau of Police for Morristown,
  67

L

Legislation and international treaties
  antihomeless ordinances, 63–67
  Emergency Relief and Construction Act,
    53
  Housing Act of 1949, 54
  Housing and Community Development
    Act of 1974, 54
  Housing and Community Development
    Amendments, 54
  Housing and Urban Development Act, 54
  Housing and Urban-Rural Recovery Act
    of 1983, 54
  HUD Reform Act of 1989, 54
  McKinney Homeless Assistance Act,
    3–4, 54–55, 79–80
  National Affordable Housing Act, 54
  National Housing Act Amendments, 53
  National Industrial Recovery Act, 53
  Personal Responsibility and Work
    Opportunity Reconciliation Act, 36, 75
  Social Security Act of 1935, 2
Libraries, 67
Living situations, 6*t,* 48–51
Local antihomeless ordinances, 63–67
Local control of assistance programs, 36–37
Loitering, 64*t*–65*t,* 66

M

Malnutrition, 73–74
Marital status, homelessness by, 6*t*
Mason v. Tucson, 68
McKinney Homeless Assistance Act, 3–4,
  54–55, 79–80
Median income, 26*t*, 27*t*, 28
Medicaid, 78–80
Mental health, 74–75
Methodology of data collection, 4–8
Metropolitan statistical areas (MSAs), least
  affordable, 59(*t*5.3)
Miami, Florida, 67–68
Minimum wage, 39*t*
Morbidity and mortality, 69–70

N

National Affordable Housing Act, 54
National Coalition for Homeless Veterans,
  21
National Coalition for the Homeless, 9
National Commission on Severely
  Distressed Public Housing, 57–58